PORTRAIT OF THE NEW FOREST

THE *PORTRAIT* SERIES

Portrait of
THE NEW FOREST

BRIAN VESEY-FITZGERALD

ILLUSTRATED
AND WITH MAP

ROBERT HALE · LONDON

© *Brian Vesey-Fitzgerald* 1966

First published in Great Britain November 1966

Reprinted February 1969

Robert Hale & Company
63 Old Brompton Road
London S.W.7

SBN 7091 0883 4

PRINTED IN GREAT BRITAIN
BY EBENEZER BAYLIS AND SON, LTD.
THE TRINITY PRESS, WORCESTER, AND LONDON

CONTENTS

ILLUSTRATIONS

ACKNOWLEDGEMENTS

The above copyright illustrations were supplied by
the following: Eric Ashby (1, 2, 14, 15, 16, 17, 18,
19); J. Allan Cash (3, 5, 6, 7, 8, 9, 10, 11, 12, 13, 21,
22); Reece Winstone (4); Leslie D. Frisby (20, 23);
Esso Petroleum Company, Ltd. (24).

INTRODUCTION

THE title of this book, *Portrait of the New Forest*, must inevitably suggest that this is a book about the New Forest as such: a book confined to the 144 square miles or so of land contained within the official perambulation. I must make it clear at once that it is not. I have strayed far beyond the official boundaries. And I have done so deliberately.

In my youth, and perhaps as late as the outbreak of the second World War, the New Forest (the 144 square miles within the official perambulation) was an entity, separate from, divorced from, the surrounding countryside: a highly individual area with a specialized life and economy of its own. Up to the outbreak of the second World War it would have been possible to write a book about the New Forest as such, ignoring the surrounding countryside and the neighbouring towns, and to give in such a book a true and valid picture of the New Forest.

This is no longer the case. It is true that, to some (but steadily decreasing) extent, the New Forest is still a separate entity with a life of its own, a life which is individual and distinct from that of the surrounding countryside. But it is no longer possible to consider the New Forest without reference to the surrounding countryside and the neighbouring towns. Modern ease and speed of transport constricts the countryside, does so more and more severely year by year, and will continue to do so. It is no longer influences within the Forest that are paramount.

I have, therefore, included in this book not only the land which the New Forest Committee 1947, with remarkable prescience, recommended should be brought within the official perambulation, but also the neighbouring towns of Bournemouth, Christchurch, Lymington and Poole. To leave them out, to include only those 144 square miles, would now be to paint a wholly misleading portrait.

Brian Vesey-Fitzgerald

For
MYM

I

THE AVON VALLEY

It seems probable that civilized man first entered England by way of the Hampshire Avon. The first major civilization to arise in England, a civilization that was to attain European eminence during the Bronze Age, was centred on the high chalk lands of Wessex. It is difficult to appreciate this now, but these high chalk lands, these open undulating Downs—most desirable country, ideal for primitive agriculturalists and livestock herders—were not at all easy to reach. They were then virtually surrounded by heavily wooded country, forest and swamp, which afforded shelter for a number of singularly unpleasant beasts and which was wholly unsuitable for settlement. There were, in fact, only three routes by which the desirable country could be reached: all river routes. (Indeed, in those days, and until the Roman engineers had done their magnificent job of road building, the rivers were the chief means of communication and transport, the "main roads" of England: and, after the Roman occupation, it was by the rivers that the Saxons and Vikings penetrated deeply into the country.) The three "main roads" to the high chalk lands of Wessex were the Hampshire Avon, the Bristol Avon, and the Thames with its tributary, the Kennet. Of these three, the Hampshire Avon was surely the most important, being the easiest to reach from northern France and once reached leading directly to the heart of the chalk land.

And still today, of all the routes into the Hampshire forest land, for the visitor with an eye for country the Hampshire Avon is by far the best. I shall, therefore, use this ancient route, which runs pretty well through the middle of the country we are about to

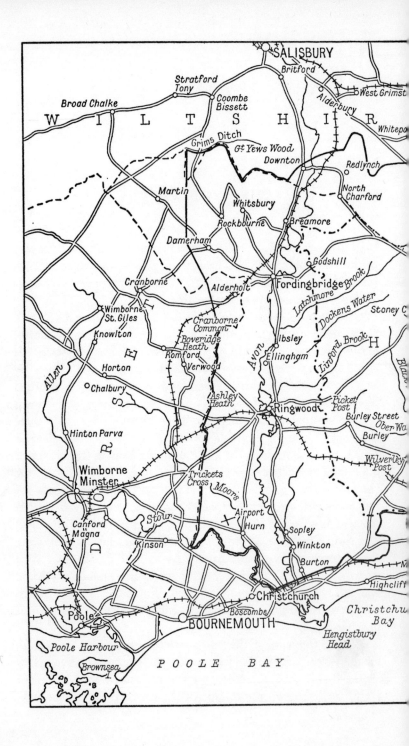

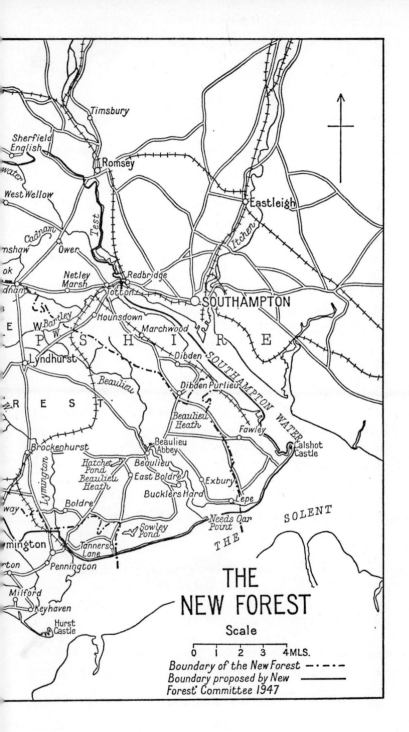

THE
NEW FOREST

Scale

0 1 2 3 4 MLS.

Boundary of the New Forest — · — · —
Boundary proposed by New
Forest Committee 1947

explore. But I shall, of course, use it in reverse, working towards the sea.

The ideal way to explore a river is to walk its bank from source to mouth, for thus you may watch it grow from childhood to maturity. Much of the Hampshire Avon lies outside the scope of this book. One joins the river in, so to speak, its middle age: at Bodenham, at the junction of Ebble and Avon, about two miles south of Salisbury. Even so, the ideal is impossible. You cannot walk beside the river, for it divides too often: you are always getting cut off by some channel or other. (I know, for I have tried: I have, indeed, walked the whole length of the Hampshire Avon.) Fortunately, the main road runs close beside the river for the whole of the twenty-six miles from Bodenham to its mouth. You are never out of sight of the water. Indeed, from Bodenham to Matrimony Farm the road runs so close to the river that it virtually forms the west bank, though there are so many channels hereabouts that it is not always easy to say which is the main stream.

A little lower down, opposite Charlton, in the woods on the little hills of the east bank, stands the eighteenth-century mansion of Standlynch, now known as Trafalgar House. The original mansion—it has been added to from time to time—was built in 1733 for Sir Peter Vandeput, a London business man. Even in those days the city tycoon had a yen for the life of the country squire, for the status symbol of the country house. In 1814 a grateful nation bestowed the mansion and the estate—and a number of other things which, gratitude having grown cold (as gratitude always does), a later government took away—on the first Earl Nelson, brother of the Admiral: hence the present name.

A couple of miles below Charlton a turning to the left takes you over the river to Downton, once a settlement within the Conqueror's New Forest and which the New Forest Committee of 1947 in their Report[1] suggested should be re-included within the perambulation. In character, Downton is certainly a Forest village and one of which I am very fond. Not that there is a great deal to see in a "tourist attraction" sense, though, if you are interested in

[1] H.M.S.O. Cmd. 7254.

Marsh marigolds in flower on Dockens Water

architecture, the church is worthy of attention and there are some fine seventeenth- and eighteenth-century houses and, in High Street, a number of nice cottages built about 1800. In the Borough an extension of High Street over the river to the west—originally this was a "new town" founded by Peter des Roches, Bishop of Winchester, in 1205—is the White Horse inn with its perpendicular niches containing heads. And there is plenty of history. The Romans were here (a seven-roomed villa and bath-house was excavated in 1955) and the Saxon hundred-moot met here. Downton's other claim to fame is that it once returned two members to Parliament, one of whom was Lord Stowell who was never known to buy a drink for himself, let alone anyone else, but who could drink any *given* quantity of port.

But Downton's appeal is not one of history, dead and long-forgotten, nor one of pleasant domestic architecture (do not be put off by the large tannery in the centre), but rather one of atmosphere, the atmosphere of a quiet backwater, to which, of course, the pleasant architecture of a more leisurely age contributes in no small measure. The main road on the west of the river carries the traffic in ceaseless procession from Salisbury to Bournemouth. Few bother to take the left-hand turn; few, I suspect, even notice it. There is a sense of peace; enhanced by the great width of the Borough. (Presumably the two long rows of houses once faced each other across a green?) And in Downton is an old coaching inn, The Bull, one of my favourite pubs.

It has always struck me as an extraordinary thing that the guide books should invariably tell you that the first place to visit in any town or village is the church. You will, of course, learn a little of the history of a place from its church, if that church is sufficiently ancient, but what you will learn is the history of a squire or two, maybe of a crusade, the history of the gentry, and a little of architecture, if you have leanings that way: all of it already in the guide book. You will learn little or nothing of the life of the place and its people. But, if you go to the inn, you will.

Well, that remark must now be qualified. Once it was true of all inns: no longer is it true of the vast majority of inns situated on main roads, for they have been "discovered" and have become

2

The Forest in early morning at Linwood

roadhouses. Most of them have a "good pull-in" for cars, a slot-machine or two, a juke-box that blares out the latest Merseyside cacophony, and a large clientele. The lounge bar (the public bar is quite likely to be empty) will be full of young men trying not to look like men and of young women trying to look like men, full of platinum blondes and over-made-up brunettes and strawberry wigs, full of bright young things in trousers (so few women are built for trousers), full of all that queer world that cannot sit still, that must be forever rushing madly from place to place, that thinks it is the "thing" to drive out to some public house to drink: not because they need the drink, not even because they like the drink, but because this is what is done on the films or on the "telly". And, curiously enough, nearly all these young women look, vaguely, like film stars. Tinned reproductions, mainly in hair style, they lounge about the bar like rows of rather lustful sardines, and the air is full of "darlings" as synthetic as their owners' complexions. Such places are no longer pubs, can no longer aspire to the noble title of "local".

Having made the necessary qualification, let me return. If you want to learn about a place, its life and its people, go not to the church, not to the parson, not to the squire, but to the inn. And go not to the lounge bar, but to the public bar. There half a pint of bitter will be sufficient passport for the whole of the lunch-time hour; for an evening, if you feel so inclined. The public bar of a village inn is a repository of folk-memory.

It is often said that it is the landlord that makes the pub. I do not believe this to be true. It is certainly true that a landlord can ruin his pub and very quickly at that, and I suppose that, once ruined, a new landlord must remake and that will be a long, hard road. But normally a good landlord does not make his pub: he maintains it. I have had many a drink in "The Bull" and many a snack over a period of many years (they must number more than forty now) and many landlords. In that time there have been improvements, of course, and now the place has been modernized, but through all the years and all the landlords, the traditional atmosphere of friendly hospitality has been maintained. I like Downton particularly just because of "The Bull".

Downton is right on the border of Hampshire. As soon as you are over the border and into Hampshire the country becomes much more heavily wooded on the east bank of the river. Within the space of a few yards the whole character of the countryside has changed. You are on heathland now, the great heathland that embraces the New Forest, the heathland that gave Thomas Hardy his background.

> Yon heathy hill
> That rises from the vale so green,
> The vale far stretching as the view can reach
> Under its long dark ridge, the river here
> That, like a serpent, through the grassy mead
> Winds on.

Southey's poem, "For the Banks of the Hampshire Avon", may not be among his best, but he knew this country well. Northward of here, the hills are light. You look at the crest of a ridge in Wiltshire and it is light-seeming, even on a dark day. You look at the crest of a ridge here and it is dark-seeming, even on a bright day. You are in the same valley, but you are beyond the influence of the chalk and into a different world. Of all the main routes into the Hampshire forest land this is by far the most revealing, so striking is the contrast it provides.

Once in Downton it is better to keep to the east bank, to take the minor road to Woodgreen, for this keeps closer to the river than does the main road. In recent years Downton has expanded down this road, but it has done so in a manner not wholly out of keeping with its centre: one is not horrified as one is by so much of modern "fringe development". At Woodgreen, an undistinguished village on the confines of the New Forest proper, turn right on to the Breamore—"Bremmer" is the correct local pronunciation—road. Cross the blue ribbon of the main Bournemouth road and you are on a wide, open green with a shallow brook running across it, and a pool where the cattle gather of an evening. Beyond the green, next to the big house, stands the village church: and this should, on no account, be missed. For this is a Saxon church, dating from the latter half of the tenth century, and still recognizably Saxon. The walls are made of whole flints and are three feet thick. The tower was originally supported on four arches and one of these, which the experts agree dates from the late tenth century, remains, with its curious lettering and cable moulding. The lettering, which was done not later than 1016, reads, it is said, "Here is manifested the Word unto thee." But only an expert could decipher that and, needless to say, there is some disagreement among the experts. Seven Saxon windows remain and there is also a very battered stone rood over the south doorway. The figures are a little more than life-size, but at the Reformation they were cut back level with the wall face, so that now only the outlines can be seen. Above the rood is a representation of the Hand of God emerging from the clouds, which are depicted by short waves. This is one of the very few specimens of ancient sculpture in this country which modern experts are prepared to accept unreservedly as Saxon. Of course, there is some later work in the building—one would expect that—but in the main this is the original fabric. And the whole is most beautifully kept.

Two miles south of Breamore is Fordingbridge. Fordingbridge, historically, is very, very old. You would never think so to look at it. There is practically nothing old-world about it, except the medieval bridge with its seven arches. The large and dignified church is actually seven hundred years old, but it has been much (and well) restored and now the most noteworthy things about it are the roof of the Lady Chapel, a beautiful example of medieval craftsmanship, and the handsomely-carved Royal Arms of George I over the north doorway. For the rest, Fordingbridge is modern; a small town of villas and bungalows and neat gardens.

This is an angler's town. The Avon cannot compare, anywhere in its length, with the Test or the Itchen as a trout stream, but from Fordingbridge southwards it boasts the best salmon fishing of any southern river and pretty well of any river in England. I have known more than one fish of 40 pounds and over taken from the Avon. But it is as a pike water that it is really famous. The pike do not run to the size of the fish of the Irish loughs, of course: nothing near that. But there are a great many large pike in this river, and twenty pounders are not considered particularly re-

markable. Indeed, the record rod-caught English pike, a fish of
37½ pounds, was taken at Fordingbridge. As a coarse fishing water
the Avon hereabouts is without rival in Britain. Quite apart from
pike, roach, dace, perch, chub, all grow to a large size. Most of the
really heavy chub, fish of 7 pounds and over (with the record for
the river standing at 8 pounds 4 ounces) are caught on the Avon.
A dace of 1 pound 8¼ ounces has been taken and dace around 1
pound 4 ounces are not uncommon. The roach run large too (a
fish of 3 pounds 10 ounces heads the list) and perch of around 4
pounds are not as uncommon as a glance at the records of heavier
fish would suggest. And in recent years some very heavy barbel,
including two equalling the British record and several over 14
pounds, have been taken. The barbel was introduced into the
Avon about the year 1900 by an Irishman, but it is only within
the last thirty years that the full effect of that enthusiast's initiative
has been appreciated, and he did not live to enjoy the fruits of his
imagination. Which is one of the saddest fishing stories I know.

When I was a boy, fishing on the Avon was easy. You just
turned up and fished. Even for the salmon it was not so very
difficult to get a day, and if you had to pay it was not very expensive. For coarse fish you could just hop over from the heart of the
Forest without even warning anyone that you were coming, get
down to the water, and fish. If you liked you could hire a boat,
and that was not beyond the pocket of a schoolboy on holiday.
Times have changed. I do not know what the salmon-fishing costs
now: I have not bothered to ask, for I know well that I have not
got that sort of pocket. Nor is the coarse fishing as free and easy
as it used to be. The boatmen have long since realized that London
business men are not so clever as they like to make out, that it is
much easier to milk a city tycoon than it is to winkle a tanner out
of a New Forest man. And I would be the last person to blame
them for grasping what the gods present.

But you can still watch the fish. It is pleasant on a warm day to
lie and watch the pike, great green monsters, so close below you
that it seems you could touch them. It is inadvisable to try. There
is a story, possibly apocryphal, of a honeymoon couple who went
for a row. The girl lay in the boat, trailing her hand in the water.

There was a swirl, the surface never broken, and a cry; and she was minus two fingers—just like that. One of those fingers bore her engagement ring and her wedding ring as decoration. About three years later a pike of 28 pounds was taken on a plug, and when opened up there were the two rings. And they got her address out of the visitors' book and sent them back to her. I will not swear to that story. But it is certainly wiser just to watch. Once, when I was a boy, I saw a big pike swimming slowly past and held crosswise in his mouth was a small pike.

All the way, so far, the valley has not been above a mile wide at any point, but below Fordingbridge it broadens considerably and you pass into quiet agricultural country. The land on both sides of the river is low hereabouts, but you get the impression that the widening of the valley is all on the west bank. The ground seems to rise to the east. And, in fact, except for the gap at Mockbeggar, leading through to Ibsley Common and the Docken Water, it does do so; but the rise is really only a few feet. The highest point on the east bank of the river between Fordingbridge and Ringwood is only some two hundred feet above sea-level. Yet that height, by comparison with the lack of height on the other bank, is sufficient to mislead entirely. And the impression is coloured yet more by the nature of the country. To the east it seems much wilder, and is in fact much wilder, than to the west.

Just south of Fordingbridge the Ditchend Brook comes into the Avon from the bare country of Ashley Walk. A gentle little stream, red-brown and placid, holding plenty of nice dace, the Ditchend Brook would hardly seem to add to the waters of what has now become a full-sized river. Yet, with only the Allen River coming in from the west at Fordingbridge itself, the Avon has grown hugely in the half-mile or so from the town. A mile and a half further south the Latchmore joins the main stream, running down from Island Thorns and the high ground by Eyeworth. A bigger water than the Ditchend Brook—I have seen it looking quite angry at times—the Latchmore, like all Forest streams, is red-brown and it holds some nice, small trout. Again the Avon seems to gain, surprisingly, quite a fair amount of water. And the story is repeated once again with Dockens Water, the largest of the three, which comes down from Fritham. Between Fordingbridge and Ellingham the Avon gathers to itself a good deal of water in a quiet way. And between Ellingham and Ringwood the Linford Brook, coming down from Broomy Walk, adds more than one would imagine. By the time Ringwood is reached the Avon has grown out of all knowledge and has, moreover, changed its character completely. These little Forest streams are, indeed, misleading. You come across them almost by accident, without warning. They are shallow and narrow, for the most part red-brown in colour and placid in temperament. There is really little to suggest that they are more than grown-up ditches. But follow them to their mouths! The Lymington River, which you can jump without undue effort at Brockenhurst, is, four miles further south, big enough to carry the Isle of Wight packet boats; and bigger boats than that if necessary. The Beaulieu River, which you can jump so comfortably at Dibden, suddenly becomes a big stream a mile or so further down its course and within another mile is a biggish river carrying fair-sized yachts. The fact is that these little Forest streams carry a great deal of water. And then, of course, there are any number of little rills—nameless all of them, and most of them too small even for mention on the Ordnance Survey map—that wind through rushy bottoms to join the Avon, and each one contributes more water than a casual glance would indicate. With every mile now, with every half-mile, the Avon seems to become deeper, to flow more purposefully. It has become much quieter too, and that adds yet more dignity. But it still has many side-runners. I have heard this stretch of the river, from Fordingbridge to the sea, compared with the Warwickshire Avon and I have heard it compared with the Thames. I think that there is in the character of the water a likeness to the Thames, and in the shape of the stream there is, perhaps, a little of the Warwickshire stream, but the Hampshire Avon has a character all its own. It is a chalk-stream proper in the number of side-runners it supports, but it is a coarse-fish river in the true tradition in the depth of its waters and the steady unhurried purpose of its flow. There is, indeed, no other river in all Britain like it. I think myself that the nearest approach is the Arun in Sussex, the Arun above Arundel; in the quality of the water, that is, and the nature of the stream. But the country-side bordering the two is, of course, quite different. And the Arun, though much swifter—it is an astonishingly swift stream—is but a child compared with the Avon.

In the seven miles between Fordingbridge and Ringwood there is but one small village and a hamlet, Ibsley and Ellingham. Ibsley church, rebuilt about 1832, is small and ugly. But it is worth a visit to see a large and beautifully sculptured wall monument, said to be the work of Epiphanius Evesham, who was born in 1572. The monument, dated 1627, commemorates Sir John Constable and his wife. The pair are kneeling and looking suitably devout. Above them, peering from a vine, are the faces of their five children, four boys and a girl: they look more than a little astonished. At one time this memorial was painted—I can remember the vine green and the fruit purple—but it is no longer so. I suppose that in these days it would be too much trouble to maintain.

Ellingham is another matter. Here is a beautiful little church, most lovingly cared for. (There is modern storage heating and strip lighting: not at all what one would expect to find in so small and isolated a place.) The building is chiefly Early English, but the south porch was rebuilt in 1720 and the west end in 1747, both in brickwork. In the gable of the porch is a remarkable, painted sundial. The altar-rails are eighteenth century and the reredos is attributed to Grinling Gibbons. At the west end is a small picture of the Last Judgement (both men and women nude and remarkably well-developed) by the Flemish painter Golzius (1558–1617). This is the sort of picture one would normally expect to find in an art gallery, not in the tiny church of a Hampshire hamlet. How did it get here? It was taken ("looted" would be the correct word) from a church in Cadiz when that town was sacked by Admiral Lord Windsor in 1702. You sometimes find history in strange places.

And there is more history here. In the churchyard, close to the south wall of the nave, is a massive chest tomb, inscribed (the lettering is now almost illegible): "Here lieth Dame Alicia Lisle and her daughter Ann Hortell who died 17 day Feb 1702. Alicia

Lisle dyed the second Sept 1685." That brief inscription commemorates a tragic and terrible story. Alicia Lisle, the wife of one of
the judges of Charles I, the judge who is said to have drawn up
the form of sentence that was read to the King, lived at Moyles
Court and worshipped in this church. She was seventy-one when
she died and she died because she gave shelter to two men after
the battle of Sedgemoor: one a dissenting minister named John
Hickes and the other a young man named Nelthorp, both of
whom had fought in the battle on the side of Monmouth. She was
betrayed by someone in the hamlet. She was arrested, together
with the two men, by a Colonel Penruddock, who was undoubtedly delighted to have the job, for thirty years earlier Judge Lisle
had sentenced his father, John Penruddock, to death as a traitor.
Alicia Lisle was tried by Judge Jeffreys at the Bloody Assize at
Winchester. She swore that she had known Hickes only as a dissenting minister, that she did not know Nelthorp's name until he
was arrested, that she had no idea that either had taken part in
Monmouth's rebellion. But Jeffreys was in his best form as judge
and prosecutor. The scene in Winchester Great Hall has been described often enough: the astonishment as the foul-mouthed judge
raved at the old lady, the muttering of the Hampshire gentlemen,
the movement of one of them to protect her (an action for which
he paid with his life), the refusal of the jury to bring in a verdict of
guilty, the rage of the judge and the threats by which he finally
forced them to change their minds and their verdict. Once he had
secured the verdict he wanted, Jeffreys sentenced Alicia Lisle to be
drawn on a hurdle to the place of execution and there burned alive:
and he directed that the sentence be carried out that very afternoon. But Hampshire refused point-blank to carry out such a
sentence, and Jeffreys dared not enforce it. He had had one rather
unpleasant experience coming through the New Forest and as a
result, even though he could bully and browbeat the Hampshire
squires, he had something of respect for the determination of the
ordinary Hampshire folk. The execution of Alicia Lisle was post-
poned for five days because the Bishop and clergy of Winchester
intervened at the judge's lodgings in the presence of a large, silent,
obviously threatening, crowd of Hampshire countrymen. For

once in his life Judge Jeffreys was frightened. But pleas to the
King were of no avail. The King (perhaps remembering his
father's death) was adamant: Dame Lisle must die. But another
sentence was substituted, for he was told bluntly that the original
one would bring all Hampshire to arms. On 2nd September 1685
Alicia Lisle, frail and ill, stepped quietly from an upper window of
the Eclipse Inn in Winchester Square, hard by the Cathedral, on
to the block and was beheaded. Her body was carried back to
Ellingham, accompanied all the way by hundreds of men on foot:
a triumphal procession rather than a funeral cortège.

Four years later a special Act of Parliament annulled the con-
viction on the ground that the verdict was "procured by the
menaces and violences and other illegal practices of Lord Jeffreys".

A couple of miles to the south of Ellingham the wandering
streams of Avon unite to form what was once a lake and is now a
shallow, soggy depression. And here, too, is a great junction of
roads: the roads from Christchurch and Poole (there is no direct
road from Bournemouth, for the simple reason that there was no
Bournemouth when these roads were fashioned) and the Forest
road from Romsey. Here, naturally, is Ringwood.

It is a very pleasant little place. There is no suggestion of great
age, though the town is of course very old, but the houses (except,
as one would expect, some of the recent, fringe building) are in
character—there is an occasional old window, weathered tiles, old
gables, some thatch—and the streets are narrow and the old
market square (there is a good modern market) intriguingly
irregular in shape. And above it all, the battlemented tower of the
church suggests at first sight that there is a castle here. In fact, the
church, a thirteenth-century foundation, was entirely rebuilt only
a little more than a hundred years ago. I find it a disappointing
building, but inside there is a somewhat mutilated but still magnificent brass—it is on the floor behind the choir stalls on the
south side of the chancel and can easily be missed, if you do not
know where to look—of John Prophete, one of the leading
churchmen of his time, who was Dean of Hereford from 1393 to
1407 and Dean of York from 1407 until his death in 1416. That
brass, rather than the church itself, is well worth a visit.

Ringwood lies some two miles outside the present Forest boundary. It was, of course, within the Conqueror's New Forest and it has always been very closely associated with the Forest. In my youth, despite its situation outside the boundary, it was very much a Forest town, spiritually as much a part of the life of the Forest as any of the genuine Forest villages of the time: a solid, rather sleepy, but undeniably prosperous, little market town. The increase in motor traffic altered all this. Its situation at the junction of three main roads saw to that. A great deal of the atmosphere, the atmosphere of a Forest town catering chiefly for Forest people, disappeared. The change was particularly noticeable in the shops, most of which, in summer at any rate, set out to capture the "chance" trade. The "chance" trade is notoriously fickle. The smaller shops tended to change hands with increasing frequency. The town developed an air of instability. Now, the traffic is carried round the town and much of the old atmosphere has returned. But I can remember, especially when the new road carrying A31 round the town was being built, that there was a good deal of apprehension among the local tradespeople at the prospect of loss of business. The reverse has, surely, been the case. For, now, people come into Ringwood, as they did formerly, because they want to, for a purpose (which, nine times out of ten, is to shop), and not just because the road carries them there.

Not that people go to Ringwood only to shop. This is also a fishing town and fishing is regarded here, as it is at Fordingbridge, as a tourist amenity. There is a local passion as well, of course. There are fishing clubs here and there are men here who seem to spend most of their lives on the banks, who know stretches of this river as well as they know the backs of their hands, who will conjure fish from the water under conditions which spell "blank day" for the expensively geared visitor. But it is the "amenity" aspect that really matters, for this brings money into the town. And this is also a fishing-match town. When a really big competition is staged men come from Birmingham, Bristol, London, Manchester, Sheffield, all over the country. Then the banks are lined with oddly-garbed men grimly determined to enjoy a day's fishing. There is an art in match-fishing, of course, though this is not apparent to the casual onlooker, and there must also be enjoyment to be had from it, though this too is not apparent to the casual onlooker: one is more impressed by the air of grim dedication. Presumably they relax afterwards.

From Ringwood the main road to Christchurch keeps to the east of the river. It runs through a flat featureless valley through which the Avon corkscrews all over the place, sometimes running in at least a dozen channels, and every now and again spreading out to form small, shallow lakes or larger rush-hidden swamps. This is a great place for birds and I have spent many hours in winter watching them. In hard weather particularly all sorts of waders come up from the shore, sometimes as far as Bisterne Park, but usually not above Avon Tyrrell. The fact that Hurn, on the west side of the river opposite Sopley, is no longer a hamlet but an airport, the fact that there is a big aircraft industry in the neighbourhood, has made no difference at all to the birds. They have become as accustomed to the noise of aircraft as we have.

Sopley is a pleasant little village—beautiful in the winter when the tourist traffic is absent—and the church should be visited for two reasons. Firstly, because it stands on a little knoll from which you get a very good view of the Avon valley trees, fringing the course of the river all the way down to the estuary. And, secondly, because in the church lies the body of Lord Keane. That is now a name that means nothing to Englishmen. But Keane was the man who led the march to Kabul in 1839. England is dotted with the graves of gallant men who have been sent on ridiculous missions by the politicians in Whitehall, planning to deal with affairs they know too little about, but there can be no more bloodstained episode in all our history than this of Kabul, no more startling evidence of the effect of meddling in affairs of which you know nothing, of ignoring the advice of the man on the spot. Keane, though he knew better, did what he was told to do. He went to Kabul. But he had to leave some of his men behind to aid the British Envoy there, and the rest of his force was cut to pieces in the Khyber Pass. Here he lies in a quiet little Hampshire village, a most fortunate soldier and an eternal memorial to the wilful ignorance of the politician. How much of our history is engraved in village churches!

The road from Sopley to the Christchurch by-pass and so into Christchurch is dull, but quick. A better, if slightly longer, way is to go back from Sopley and take the lane over the river which leads to Hurn, and then the secondary road to Christchurch. Better still, go back over the river but, before reaching Hurn, get on to the old railway track—there used to be a light railway from Christchurch to Ringwood and its track can still be followed without difficulty—and walk into Christchurch, a matter of three miles or so. The track passes through low-lying marshes, green and yellow, russet and purple, below the bluff of St Catherine's Hill and always before you the Priory rises grey from the mists of the estuary. I know of no better approach to Christchurch than this.

St Catherine's Hill. Now, that is an interesting name. Catherine was the virgin martyr of Alexandria. This young woman is reputed to have been broken on a wheel and then beheaded in the year 307. A legend grew up around her name in Syria and in due course she was canonized. The early Crusaders brought the cult to western Europe, and it reached England shortly after the Norman Conquest. (The first reference to the saint in England is in a miracle play based on her story, which was first performed at Dunstable in 1100.) In 1148 Queen Matilda founded a collegiate church and hospital, dedicated to her, near the Tower of London. There is nothing like royal patronage for giving a cause a boost. From that date the cult of St Catherine spread, albeit slowly, through the country, attaining its greatest popularity in the fourteenth century.

From a glance at the map it might well be thought that Hampshire was a centre, indeed the centre in all England, of the cult of this virtuous Levantine girl with the legendary powers. For there are no fewer than three landmarks in the county named St Catherine: this hill near Christchurch, St Catherine's Hill near Winchester, and St Catherine's Hill in the Isle of Wight. (Indeed, there is a fourth, St Catherine's Point in the Isle of Wight, but that was named after the high hill behind it and at a much later date.) But the fact is that the saint was never popular in Hampshire. There is only one church in the county dedicated to her—there are sixty-four in England as a whole—and she did not give her name directly to any of these landmarks. The name is a corruption of Cader Ryn, the fort above the river. There was a fort, a strong place, on each of these hills.

It is true that there was also a chapel on each of them, but only one is known for certain to have been dedicated to St Catherine. This was the chapel on St Catherine's Hill in the Isle of Wight. There was a hermitage on this hill. In the registers of the diocese there is this entry: "Walter de Langstrell admissus ad hermitorium supra montem de Chale in insula Vectis, Id. Octobris, AD 1312." From this it is evident that the hill was not then known, even to the religious, as St Catherine's. In 1323 Walter de Godyton built a chapel on the site of the hermitage and dedicated it to St Catherine. There is an obvious similarity between Cader Ryn and Catherine, and this may well have had a good deal to do with the dedication. The Christian church was never averse from taking over pagan sites and adapting them to Christian usage, and the very fact that a hermitage was situated here suggests that the place had some significance, not necessarily religious, left over from pagan times. The Isle of Wight chapel has long since disappeared, but the name remains. This hill was, I believe, the first of the landmarks to be known as St Catherine's.

The existence of a chapel on St Catherine's Hill near Christchurch is much more doubtful. There can be no doubt about the fort—the outlines of the earthworks are plainly visible—and there are a number of tumuli on the hill. But all that remains of the "chapel" is a square of fifty-five yards, which is marked on large scale Ordnance Survey maps as "Site of St Catherine's Chapel." Fragments of worked Purbeck marble have been found here and the marks of what were obviously foundations have been found in the centre. But the square is surrounded by a low bank and a ditch, and this does not suggest that a chapel was to be built. In any case, there is no record of any dedication. If there ever was a chapel on this hill, it was never dedicated: it was simply the chapel on Cader Ryn.

The local legend is that it was never intended to build a chapel on the hill, but a church; and that it was not built because each night essential stones were removed by some unknown hand and transferred to a place about a mile to the south. After this had happened several times the local builders took the hint, abandoned the hill, and started building at the place indicated. Immediately the workmen were joined by another, a model workman who worked hard all day, but was never present at mealtimes and never drew any pay. One day, when the church was almost completed, it was found that one of the beams was a foot too short. The strange workman placed his hand upon it and, instantly, it fitted. Thereafter the strange workman was seen no more. At this time the place was known as Twynham, but now, at the workmen's demand, it was named Christchurch, for the carpenter's Son had had a hand in the building of it. The same legend, except for the beam part of it, occurs in many other places, though the casting down and removal of the originally planned church is usually credited to the devil.

I have a great fondness for Christchurch Priory, so clean and fresh and lovingly cared-for, and particularly for its situation. (Really, you should stand on Hengistbury Head to get the proper view of the Priory, for then only do you realize to the full why it is called the Priory in the Marsh.) And there is always that miracle to think about, and the way that it made Flambard, William Rufus's unscrupulous justiciar, feel holy all of a sudden. Though, in fact, I am not sure that it made him feel anything of the sort: I feel pretty sure that such a man realized that there was money in miracles. Flambard was a rogue beyond question, but he was a genius at this business of church building. You have only to consider Durham Cathedral to understand how great a genius. And certainly he sited this Priory Church ideally.

As a church it is difficult to describe: and I do not intend to try, for there are so many excellent guides to it. What has always struck me about it—and I have been in it more times now than I count—is that it is not a whole in any sense, except when viewed from a distance. It might best be described as a catalogue of the English styles of architecture, a collection of samples. But it is a collection which includes only good work. Particularly fine is the Norman turret at the east end of the north transept. The great north porch must be one of the finest examples of Early English work to be seen anywhere in the country; the windows in the south aisle are good Decorated; the rood-screen, a glorious example of the stone-mason's art, is beautiful Perpendicular. And so you could go on. Christchurch Priory to be appreciated as it deserves to be must be seen many times, each visit being devoted to the study of one portion. And each visit should also include a distant view of the whole—from Hengistbury Head.

Quite apart from the Priory, Christchurch itself rewards leisurely exploration. There is more in modern Christchurch than meets the casual eye. For example, the broad High Street with its modern shop fronts and multiple stores is just like any other modern High Street if you look only at the shop windows. But if you look up—how few people do!—you will see steep old roofs and gable ends, dormer windows, Tudor windows, and some beautiful bow windows dating from Queen Anne and early Georgian times. But I think that the best thing to do is to take the short walk recommended by the local council's guide book. There is a map of the route in the local guide book, and the walk does not take more than twenty minutes; though, if you are wise, you will dawdle (you will find it very difficult not to!) and spin it out to an hour. If you cannot spare the shilling for the guide book— it is one of the best local guides I know, for it has been compiled with love and with a strict regard for historical truth (an attribute rarer in local guides than you might imagine), and is worth every penny of the twelvepence asked—then start from the King's Arms Hotel, walk down Convent Walk—to begin with you walk between the River Avon and the ruins of the Constable's House (though ruined, still a fine and rare example of twelfth-century domestic architecture) and then between a boat-builder's yard and the Priory—to the Norman bridge and Christchurch Quay, then up Quay Road and through the churchyard to Church Street, turn right into Castle Street, past the Castle Mound, and so back to the King's Arms. It is a short walk, but it gives you the full flavour of Christchurch: the old and the new, the busy and

Sunset and swans. The River Avon at Fordingbridge

the quiet. And I think you will fall in love with the town, as I do anew every time I go there and take this walk, which I always make a point of doing.

At Christchurch the Stour comes into the estuary from the Dorset uplands, forming a great stretch of water that once was a famous harbour. A good deal of our history started here. These south-coast rivers formed gateways into England; and the Avon was not the least important of them. The Hallstart culture of the Iron Age may, perhaps, have come into the country by this route. Certainly, it was well-established here: its deeply-incised and fine haematite-coated wares have been found in some profusion on Hengistbury Head. And the fort on the Head was not put there for no purpose at all. It is magnificently sited for defence, the narrow neck cut by the ditches, the expanse of Christchurch behind making it almost impregnable. There can, I think, be little doubt that at that time this was an important port from which goods were exported to the Continent. Later invaders also came this way. Hengist, on his second invasion, landed here (hence Hengistbury Head), and no doubt it remained a port usable by the small ships of those days for many years.

Now, it is no longer a port and the word "harbour" is but a courtesy title. The time when these south-coast rivers were the channels of commerce has long since passed. Once goods were carried far inland and the produce of the countryside were brought to the ports by their means. Changed conditions of transport have altered the use that is made of rivers today. But the main factors in the decay of these southern rivers have been the wind and the weather, and the silt. In many cases these potent forces have blocked outlet to the sea altogether—Winchelsea is a good example of a former port now landlocked—in many others have rendered the rivers unnavigable. In Hampshire the rivers have been lost to the merchant: they have become the playground of the fisherman. At Christchurch the harbour is now shut off from the sea by a sandbank that has formed through the centuries. The combined waters of Stour and Avon now find their way to the sea at Mudeford through a narrow channel, known as "The Run". This sandbank has made of the harbour a great lagoon, what is

3

Ruins of the Constable's House at Christchurch

virtually a huge salt-water lake, and this is much enjoyed by sailing enthusiasts.

From time to time proposals have been made for opening up Christchurch Harbour again. John Taylor, after making a journey by boat from London to Salisbury in 1623, wrote in his *New Discovery by Sea* of the trade that could be brought into Salisbury by water if Christchurch Harbour was open. As a result an Act was passed in 1644 for making the river navigable. But nothing was done. In 1674 Andrew Yarranton, in his *England's Improvement*, said that he had been taken down the Avon by Lord Clarendon to see if a safe harbour could be made at Christchurch. He recommended that a great harbour be constructed, and work was actually started, for a pier and a wharf were built shortly afterwards. But, again, nothing came of it. Not long afterwards we find Defoe writing: "As for Christchurch, tho' it stands at the mouth of the Avon, which, as I have said, comes down from Salisbury, and brings with it all the waters of the north part of Dorsetshire; yet it is a very inconsiderable, poor place, scarcely worth seeing." Now it is much too late to do anything. The silting is going on all the time, and one day the lake will be a lake in the full sense, and the waters will seep out through the sands. And it is better this way. It is a beautiful lagoon and a source of much profit to the ancient town of Christchurch.

Between Christchurch and Mudeford—a fishing village with some good Georgian houses which, because it is still a fishing village (salmon are netted in "The Run"), retains a character distinctive from that of the ordinary seaside resort—lies Stanpit Marsh, one of the famous places on the south coast for birds and particularly for waders. Almost every rare wader on the British list has been seen here at some time or another. A visit to Stanpit Marsh is always an excitement, for you never know what you may see.

II

THE BOURNEMOUTH HEATHLAND

I APPLY the name, for want of a better, to that area of land which lies between the Stour and the sea, bounded on the east by Hengistbury Head and Christchurch Harbour and on the west by Poole Harbour and the main road (A349) from Poole to Wimborne Minster. With the exception of the ancient heart of Poole, this roughly triangular area of land was, until quite recently, heathland and exceptionally poor and barren heathland at that; as desolate a region as could be found anywhere in England, a vast and treeless heath, intersected here and there by narrow gorges (the old Hampshire name for these was "bunnies", but they are now known as "chines"), and virtually unpopulated.

At the beginning of the last century there was the ancient Borough of Poole (its Charter of Incorporation dates from 1248) at the head of its almost landlocked harbour, and then, all the way along the coast as far as Christchurch, no settlement at all, save for some half-dozen fishermen's cottages at the mouth of the little Bourne stream. Maybe, at that time, no more than a score of people lived along the coast between Christchurch and Poole. It is difficult to believe that now. Now, save for a small piece at the western end, inland of Holes Bay, it is one vast built-up area. To-day more than a quarter of a million people live permanently within this triangle; and many many more during the summer months. Today, the rateable value of Poole is £4,824,126: that of Bournemouth £9,704,430. It needs a seeing-eye to recognize the heathland now.

"We have remarked", wrote Spencer Thomson in 1860 in his *Health Resorts of Great Britain; How to Profit by Them*, "that places like Folkestone, which, but a few years ago were a mere collection of huts, have partly owing to their own capabilities, and partly under the care of the Railway Companies, sprung up into well-frequented and well-appointed watering-places; but Bournemouth has sprung from nothing as it were, for as late as the commencement of the present century, its site was not simply unfrequented, but, to all intents and purposes uninhabited, except by the wild fowl."

It all began, this quite fantastic story, with the Enclosure Act of 1801: an Act designed to promote the cultivation of waste land as a means of increasing the national wealth. As a result of that Act someone (nobody now knows who he was) began planting pine trees on the desolate Bournemouth heathland. Yes, even the pines for which Bournemouth is famous are a comparatively modern introduction: though perhaps, to be strictly accurate, one should say "re-introduction", for these pine trees flourish where pine forests grew in prehistoric times, as fossil remains on the fore-shore prove beyond question. In 1810 Mr Lewis Tregonwell, a middle-aged gentleman, happened to be staying with his young wife at Mudeford, then a small and very select watering-place, and one day they drove in their own "chariot" over the heath to the Bourne Chine. Mrs Tregonwell instantly fell in love with the place and said that she would like to live there. She was a new wife and Mr Tregonwell saw no reason why she should not have whatever she wanted. He had the money—he was, indeed, a wealthy man—and land was available. He bought the land and built a marine villa, which he called The Mansion, on the site where now stands the Exeter Hotel. And he set about beautifying the place by making a decoy pond and planting a great many pines up and down the chine. Mrs Tregonwell was delighted. But not for long. There were no other houses; only half-a-dozen fishermen's cottages. There were no houses nearer than Poole on the one hand, Christ-church on the other: there was no company. Mrs Tregonwell soon began to feel lonely. So Mr Tregonwell set about persuading some of his relatives to buy and build along the chine, and then a few of his friends. He must have been a persuasive man, for when he died in 1832 there were six large houses scattered along the chine and a few more cottages too: built, presumably, for the out-door staff needed by the new residents.

But if it was Lewis Tregonwell who, at the instigation of his young wife, gave birth to Bournemouth, it was an astute business man, Sir George Tapps Gervis, who realized that here was the nucleus of a resort and immediately set about exploiting the possibilities to the full. Sir George, if he had an eye to the main chance—as undoubtedly he had; and who would blame him for that?—was also a man of vision. He looked at the solid, comfortable houses already there, each secluded in its own grounds, and determined that his should be a resort with a difference; that he would develop on Tregonwell lines. But first he built an hotel, a boarding house, a library and reading-room, and he bought two of the cottages, knocked them together, and turned them into a chapel. He now had the essentials of a resort, and set about publicizing it. Almost at once we find the *Hampshire Advertiser* informing its readers that "the new romantic watering-place called Bourne is progressing at railway speed". The essential requisites of a watering-place achieved, Sir George set about building a "marine village" of tasteful villas in the Elizabethan, Gothic, Greek and Italian styles along the cliff. By 1838 he was advertising "furnished and papered villas with every requisite" at four guineas a week. That was a very considerable sum for those days. The new resort was to be as select as price could make it. The policy was a success. In 1842 we read of "Bournemouth where in a season, the magic hand of enterprise has converted the silent and unfrequented vale into the gay resort of fashion, and the favoured retreat of the invalid" and of "detached villas, indicating every variety of style that the fancy and ingenuity of the architect could devise . . . rows of stately edifices, relieved by the dark foliage of dense plantations . . . the whole softened by an air of tranquil repose and a quietude of character eminently grateful to those who seek relaxation from the fatigue and excitement of fashionable life, or a respite from the turmoils and anxieties of rough inter-course with the world."

In a matter of ten years Sir George had done remarkably well. Now he was to set the seal on his achievement. He invited Dr

Granville to his new resort and persuaded him—not that he would have needed much persuasion—to speak at a public dinner. Dr Granville was *the* fashionable doctor, one of the most sought-after medical men of the day, a man of enormous influence. It is apparent from his writings that he was an appalling snob, an unctuous toady to the rich, and an expert on women, with a bedside manner that charmed the guineas from the ladies. Inevitably, since he specialized in the ailments of the wealthy, he was also a specialist on watering-places. If he were to give the new resort his blessing, then the place would be made.

Dr Granville made an exceptionally long speech—you will find it reprinted in full in his *Spas and Principal Sea-Bathing Places*—too long unfortunately (for it has some delightful touches) to quote in full. He began by praising the "balsomic effluvia" of the pine forests which made, he said, Bournemouth the ideal place for consumptives. He then went on to tell the company how the new resort should be developed. He had been given a plan of the proposed new development—one cannot escape the impression that this plan did not meet with the full approval of Sir George Gervis and that the good doctor had been thoroughly briefed by his host on the matter—and, holding up this plan, he proceeded to give a solemn warning: "If this engraving is likely to be realized, then Bournemouth will become one of twenty watering-places, just as tolerable and common, and will only be frequented as such, with slow progress and doubtful success." He urged them not to allow "mere brick-and-mortar speculators . . . to build up whole streets of lodging houses, or parades and terraces interminable, in straight lines facing the sea, the roaring sea, and the severe gales, that make the frames of an invalid's bedroom casement rattle five days in the week at least, and shake his own frame in bed also." He went on to point out that such "terraces, parades, paragons and parabolas of houses of every sort and description . . . acted on the influx of the better sort of people in exactly the inverse ratio of their own increasing numbers. What the result of such a proceeding has been to the place itself I need not specify." Having made the point, pretty forcibly, he went on to suggest that the correct development would be to build "insulated villas with properly located gardens", sloping up the hill behind them, and that each villa should have its own stables, so that the people of the better sort should be able to take an outing whenever they wished. How Sir George must have approved!

Having put the building development to rights, Dr Granville proceeded to suggest development of the chine itself. He did not approve of the "miserable" sheep that grazed the banks of the stream; and he did not think much of the stream itself. He suggested "a little judicious management, so as to create a rustling fall or cascade, would readily convert an insignificant streamlet into a pleasing ornamental water-feature in the landscape". The removal of the sheep and the construction of this water-feature would, he suggested, make of the chine a very pleasant promenade-garden.

Sir George Gervis died shortly after this historic dinner. But, impressed by the Doctor's eloquence and commonsense, the surviving residents scrapped their proposed plan for development and adopted his suggestions in their stead. They saw to it that insulated villas with properly located gardens were built and that each had its own stabling: they got rid of the sheep: they made of the little Bourne brook an ornamental water-feature: they planted flower-beds and parterres, and made of the chine a pleasant promenade-garden. And Dr Granville played his part. He became the new resort's best publicity-agent, for, as Walcott says, he gave "to this sequestered village of villas without a street the preference over all the bathing-places of the south and west coasts". Bournemouth had arrived.

It was, to begin with, a sad little place. Dr Granville did his work well, and other doctors followed his lead. The consumptives, the people "dying of a decline", flocked in—to cough out their lives amid the pines and the flowers. It was not the "mere brick-and-mortar speculators" who built the original Bournemouth. It was the undertakers.

Here is the picture of Bournemouth given a few years later by Sir Walter Besant and James Rice in their *The Seamy Side*. "They planted it as a Garden of Eden. . . . Hither come, when the rest of the world is still battling with the east wind and frost, hollow-cheeked young men and drooping maidens to look for the tree of life. . . . They do not find that tree, but the air revives them for a while, and they linger on a little longer, and have time to lie in the sunshine and see the flowers come again before they die. This is the city of Youth and Death . . . Here and there you find an old man who has stumbled into the graveyard by accident. It jars upon the sense of right; it is an offence for him to have lived till seventy."

And so it was for many years after the death of Dr Granville, for the doctors continued to send their patients to cough out their lives by the seaside. The essential article of furniture in the bedrooms of Bournemouth and Torquay was the "spitting-pot". But the healthy had also come to live in the expanding Bournemouth and it was the local paper, noting this and the lack of facilities for them—the dying were not thought to require amusement—that drove the first nail into the coffin of the original Bournemouth. "It would satisfy", it said, "neither our interest nor our ambition were Bournemouth to become the very Metropolis of Bath Chairs. We desire that these may be the appendages only of a cheerful and pleasure-taking resort." That pronouncement aroused a good deal of local support. But the struggle to alter the place—and, particularly, its image in the public mind: it had acquired a great reputation as an invalid colony—was long and hard. For years after that first attack the town could not make up its mind what it wanted to be; was neither the one thing nor the other. One gets a very clear impression of this from the writings of those who lived in the town or who knew it well during the eighties. Robert Louis Stevenson, who lived here from 1884 to 1887 (it was here that he wrote *Kidnapped* and *Dr Jekyll and Mr Hyde*), described life in Bournemouth as being "as monotonous as a weevil's in a biscuit". Yeo, in his *Climate and Health Resorts*, written at about the same time, pointed out that there was "no esplanade or promenade by the sea" and went on to say that "as the place consists chiefly of private houses, scattered through the pine forest, it is found very dull by invalids who go there without their families, and without friends there". Yet Thomas Hardy, who also knew the town at this period, but who went there only as a casual visitor, for a day or two at a time, described it in *Tess of the D'Urbervilles* as a "pleasure city", "a glittering novelty", and "like a fairy palace".

Bournemouth received its Charter of Incorporation as a Borough in 1890. It was then that it finally made up its mind to push the bath chairs into the background: to become a pleasure resort. Viewed from this distance of time that decision appears to have been inevitable. At the time it most certainly could have appeared nothing of the sort. Then it was a gamble: in essence a gamble between death and life. Bournemouth, at that time, might well have secured the monopoly of the invalid trade: an undeniably profitable trade, if one concentrated, as Bournemouth did, on the well-to-do. It was no small decision to forego that possibility in favour of competition with such places as Brighton. It proved, and quickly, unbelievably quickly, to be a wise decision.

Within twenty years Moutray Read, in his *Highways and Byways in Hampshire*, could describe Bournemouth as a fashionable pleasure resort: not, mark you, as a health resort. Nevertheless, he had reservations:

So established is Bournemouth's popularity that some courage is needful to confess to have found it ever dreary and depressing! Yet when the dank sea mist wraps round the sad remnants of pine plantations, and never a mouthful of air penetrates to the shut-in valleys, it is one of the most cheerless and sombre places it has ever been my lot to live in. Even the heather looks dark and toneless, and the dripping pines can be the acme of melancholy!

Only when the sun shone did Moutray Read find Bournemouth bearable, and even then he felt forced to make comparisons not wholly to Bournemouth's advantage:

But one forgets November days when the sun floods the beautiful bay and the blue waters dance below the cliffs with their crown of golden gorse; and, though the sandy track that runs along East Cliff from the pier to Boscombe is less pleasant underfoot for a saunter than Folkestone's grassy Leas, and at the same time no freer from the trammels of fashion, you get the same fine effect of sea-scape below you, and a sunset over Poole Harbour may hold its own with one

over Sandgate Roads and Romney Marsh, for if there is no Shorn-
cliffe to rise dark above the reflected glories in the bay below, there
is—literally on the other hand—the Island with its wonderful white
cliffs and the rugged Needles to make a finish on the eastern horizon.

Well, the sandy track is asphalt now, easier (and harder!) walking;
and now no one can tell with certainty where Bournemouth ends
and Boscombe begins. But the view remains. And this view from
the cliff—looking out over Christchurch Bay, the Needles on the
one hand, Old Harry on the other—is one which no other seaside
resort in Britain can surpass.

Thirty years after Moutray Read the anonymous author of the
section on Bournemouth in Arthur Mee's *Hampshire* had no reservations whatsoever:

Millions of people know that there is no more delightful seaside
town for those who love to be in touch with nature and to see her
unspoiled. Here if we come in the busy months is an endless throng
of people winding through the Central Square, but those who know
feel that it is not unfitting that there should rest within sound of
them all the heart of the poet of the Skylark, the Winds, and the
Clouds. It is not unfitting that the heart of Shelley should lie here,
for if Bournemouth is crowded it is beautiful, fit garden to have so
precious a thing in its keeping. Its romantic chines, the little ravines
with trees and shrubs running inland from the coast, carrying sea
breezes into the streets, are unmatched anywhere, captivating places.
The far-spread spaces of Bournemouth's parks (Meyrick Park 194
acres and Queen's 175) offer an endless delight of heather, gorse,
and open common. The Overcliff Drive follows the cliffs for five
miles without a stop. The bathing beach is six miles long; it must
have been this fine stretch of golden beach that suggested Thomas
Hardy's name for Bournemouth—Sandbourne; he calls it so in *Tess*.
Where shall we find such rhododendrons in a town, where such
glorious walks for mile upon mile in a perfect natural paradise?

The little Bourne runs through a chain of gardens (miles of them)
cut through the middle of the town, growing more lively as we
approach the sea, the quiet upper gardens shaded with trees, the
tennis courts below. Then comes the noble column in memory of
Bournemouth's heroes, guarded by four lions. Trickling through a
pretty water garden, the stream plunges under the crowded Square,

the busy hub of Bournemouth, and beyond, as if it were glad to be
free from its gloomy tunnel, through a glorious rockery. We have
not seen a better laid-out pleasure space than this, ending in the grand
Pavilion with its windows looking on to the Channel. Here is the
Bourne Mouth; it pours itself into the sea under a pier a thousand
feet long. Surely this town of 140,000 people is a happy place, with
miles of sand dunes without a fisherman, a town without an industry except that of making people happy. It caters for a vast multi-
tude all the year round, and it is known to travellers everywhere as
a seaside town without a rival.

That, I feel sure, was written by a woman (no man would have
missed the fishermen, of whom there are plenty!) and a resident
of Bournemouth or its immediate environs. There is the fine
flourish of local patriotism about it. But, save for the legend of
Shelley's heart, which should be taken with a large pinch of salt
(Shelley was drowned off the coast of Italy in 1822 and was cre-
mated on the shore at the spot where his body was found), it is not
an inaccurate picture. It was not an inaccurate picture at the time
it was written and it is not an inaccurate picture now, almost
thirty years later, for Bournemouth in that period, though it has
spread considerably, has changed but little. It is, however, an in-
complete picture, for it treats of Bournemouth only as a pleasure
town, a holiday town. And Bournemouth is much more than
that.

It is true that the town has some magnificent public gardens:
as good as any in Britain and far, far better than most. It is true
that the holiday-maker is catered for here as well as anywhere in
Britain, though perhaps without the gusto that one associates with
Blackpool, Margate or Southend. But Bournemouth is also a
cultural centre. The Art Gallery and the Museum are both of a
standard not usually associated with "holiday" towns. There is,
and regularly, good music and good drama (as good as you will
get in London and presented to audiences much more comfortably seated) and the town has many societies (literary, philosophical,
and scientific, and so on) with flourishing memberships. Bournemouth is, in fact, a residential as well as a holiday town. And the
residential population, a large proportion of it made up of

"retireds", is immensely important to the town: as important, indeed, as is the holiday .trade.

This residential population lives in what is really a vast, sprawling suburb; closely contingent to, sometimes inextricably mixed with, but somehow always quite apart from, the holiday Bournemouth. This suburban Bournemouth is often described as drab and ugly. Featureless would be a better description. It is true that residential Bournemouth is rather anonymous, but it is certainly not ugly. The streets are wide and clean, and the gardens, almost without exception—Bournemouth, taking its cue from the beautiful municipal gardens, is a town of dedicated gardeners—are most colourful and most lovingly tended. It must be admitted that the architecture of residential Bournemouth is generally undistinguished. But what would one expect? Of course, there is no Regency architecture. Of course, there are no terraced gems such as Brighton and Hove can boast. The history of the place rules out anything like that. I should doubt if there are a dozen buildings in the whole of Bournemouth more than a hundred years old.

Nevertheless, remembering that Bournemouth's history is confined to a period singularly undistinguished in architectural achievement, it is astonishing how many fine public buildings of real architectural merit it can boast. Notable among them are four churches. St Peter's, the mother church of the town, built between 1855 and 1879 on the site of the original chapel of 1844, was designed by Street, the architect of the Law Courts. It ranks among the most effective examples of Street's work, though for my taste it is a little too lavishly decorated. St Michael's, on the hill towards Poole, designed by Shaw and completed in 1876, has an impressive pinnacled tower by Oldrid Scott, which was added in 1901. St Stephen's, on Richmond Hill, designed by Pearson, the architect of Truro Cathedral, and built between 1881 and 1908 (though it is not yet fully completed), is by far the most beautiful of Bournemouth's churches and, indeed, its cathedral-like interior must take high rank among modern churches anywhere in Britain. Finally, the church of St Francis of Assisi, designed by Gibbons and completed in 1929, standing on the northern edge of the town, is a remarkable replica of early Romanesque. That word "replica" is, I suppose, sufficient to damn it straightaway in the eyes of many people. But I beg you to go and see it; if possible, on a sunny day. Only on a sunny day do you get the full contrast between the colour of the roof and the square white tower and white walls: only on a sunny day do you receive the full impact of the wide, simple, starkly white interior with its coloured ceiling. The church of St Francis on a bright, sunny day is a breathtaking experience.

If it is true (and it is) that today no one can tell with certainty where Boscombe ends and Bournemouth begins—and there is, of course, no longer reason why anyone should, since the two are now one: Boscombe has been swallowed up and has altogether lost its identity—it is no less true that today no one can tell with certainty where Bournemouth ends and Poole begins. The bricks and mortar stretch on and on endlessly. Leaving Bournemouth one goes on believing that one is in Bournemouth at least until one gets a glimpse of Poole Harbour. This should, of course, be the same the other way round: leaving Poole one ought to go on believing that one is in Poole at least until one gets a glimpse of Bournemouth pier. But this is not so. The moment one loses sight of Poole Harbour one believes that one is in Bournemouth. In fact, what many people consider to be among the most desirable residential districts of Bournemouth—Branksome Park and Canford Cliffs, for example—are in Poole; not in Hampshire at all, but over the border in Dorset.

This may well sound as though Poole, like Boscombe, has been swallowed up, has lost its identity. But that is very far from being the case.

It is true that the eastern suburbs of Poole merge with the western suburbs of Bournemouth, that they are indistinguishable the one from the other. The soil is the same and the houses, even allowing for differences in period (Edwardian Red Brick, "Jerrybethan", and so on) bear a strong family likeness. You may call some of this Poole, some of this Bournemouth—you may be more specific and call some of this Branksome Park or Canford Cliffs or Parkstone—the names matter not at all. This is a land apart. This is Suburbia, Suburbia *par excellence*: extremely well-to-do, self-consciously "select", eminently desirable, withdrawn, quiet, springing to life (in summer to the sound of innumerable motor-mowers) only at the week-ends: the land of domesticity, of trim houses and neat gardens, of tennis courts and golf courses. Local government-wise much of it may be within the Borough of Poole. But, in fact, it is divorced from Poole as Southbourne, for example, is not divorced from Bournemouth. This suburbia did not grow up, as suburbs usually do, because its inhabitants worked in the neighbouring town and wished, as they grew more prosperous, to live in a more select area a little distance from their work. The original development here was not from Poole nor from Bournemouth, but by wealthy people from far away, from London and the midlands and the north, who could afford to give expression to the rural romanticism, which is present in every successful business man, and have a "country house" by the sea. Originally, there were no roots in either Bournemouth or Poole, but the pull, if any, was towards Bournemouth and its entertainments, and, beyond Bournemouth, to the open spaces of the New Forest. The people who came here came to escape. Today, the area is more truly suburbia in its strict sense (there are many people living here who do work in the neighbouring towns) and officially part of the Borough of Poole, but the leisure links are still with Bournemouth, the entertainment centre, rather than with Poole, the commercial town.

Travelling westwards from Bournemouth it is impossible to know precisely when you enter the Borough of Poole, but once you are in Poole proper there can be no doubt about it. Poole has an identity, a presence, all its own. And this is not merely a matter of commerce. Poole is, of course, a seaport and a busy one: and there are here the industries, the timber yards, the warehouses, the smells and the bustle common to seaports everywhere. Of course, this sets Poole apart from Bournemouth. But it is not this alone that sets Poole apart. Poole is also a holiday town, even if not so well known in this respect as its near neighbour, with all the trappings (except a good theatre) of a holiday town. Yet as holiday towns there is a marked difference between the two, and so in the people that visit them. And the reason for this is the harbour.

Poole Harbour is the second largest natural harbour in the world—the largest is Sydney, Australia—seven miles long and four miles broad. Its double tides ensure almost fourteen hours of high water in every twenty-four, and the tidal rise and fall is never more than six feet. These are advantages which would be sufficient to make Poole one of the great seaports of the world were it not for the fact that the harbour is almost land-locked. Moreover, there is only one deep-water channel, and that not deep enough. This and the narrow entrance restricts the harbour to ships of about 2,000 tons burthen and drawing less than twenty feet of water. But, if all this is a serious handicap commercially, it has made of Poole Harbour a paradise for the yachtsman and the small-boat enthusiast. There are no fewer than six Yacht Clubs, each with its own club house and private jetty. Membership of these clubs is eagerly sought and not always easy to obtain. Inevitably, there are some social jealousies. But these are much less obvious than in some other sailing centres I could mention, for here all the clubs are primarily sailing clubs and all make a point of encouraging young people and teaching them to sail. Indeed, there is also a Poole Youth Sailing Club.

In fact, the population of Poole is made up of four pretty distinct groups. Firstly, a resident population engaged in the commerce of the port and the town; in ship-building and marine engineering, in caravan-building (some of the best motor-caravans in the world are built here), in a multiplicity of light industries, confectionery, pottery, and so on. (A visit to Lloyds Bank and a study of the magnificent mural, made of locally produced tiles, depicting the trade of the town, is an enlightening and rewarding experience.) Secondly, a suburban population, which includes a high proportion of retired people and which, for the most part, has a natural affinity with the pleasures of Bournemouth rather than with the realities of the Borough in which it resides. Thirdly, a sailing population which comes and goes with the tides. And, fourthly, a holiday population, largely made up of families with young children and which is in a sense more permanent than one would expect, for families which once come to Poole for a holiday tend to go on doing so year after year until the children have grown up. By then many of them have become interested in sailing and so the connection continues even unto the third and fourth generation. Indeed, my personal observation has convinced me that a fair proportion of the resident retired population formed its first association with the town as young children, brought for a summer holiday by boat-minded parents. I think that Poole has a firmer hold on its holiday population than any other holiday resort in the British Isles, including Blackpool with its strong "Wakes" tradition.

Certainly the town does its best for children and their parents, catering for them as thoroughly as it does for the sailing enthusiast. Indeed, more so: for the sailing connection is a natural by-product of that wonderful inland sea, Poole Harbour. Amenities for children and their parents have been deliberately provided by a civic authority, blessed with good sense and good taste, which has been at pains to provide a relatively huge area, over a thousand acres in all, of public parks and open spaces. Of these, Poole Park is the finest both in respect of size and amenities. Sophisticated people nowadays tend to despise "public parks": heaven knows why. I suppose that it is that they are ordered, with trim flower beds and asphalt paths, not wild and natural. Well, there is any amount of the wild and natural all around: the New Forest, the islands in the harbour, the virtually uninhabited stretches of foreshore around the western edges of the harbour, as wild and isolated a country as is to be found anywhere in the south of England, miles and miles of it. Those seeking solitude can find it without difficulty. But little, if any, of this is suitable holiday ground for those with young children: Poole Park is and so is Hamworthy Park. Poole Park boasts a salt-water lake of sixty acres; surely one of the largest and certainly one of the safest boating-lakes in England. Here you may row or canoe or sail or let the children loose in paddleboats. Here, too, is a model yacht enclosure, which must be one of the best in Britain and which is always heavily patronized. Here for the children—and their fathers!—is a miniature narrow-gauge railway and a small zoo,

Norman work in Christchurch Priory

which is of a surprisingly high standard. Bowls, tennis, putting: Poole Park has everything, including the trim flower beds and the asphalt paths. Hamworthy Park, on a smaller scale, also caters particularly for children.

Both these parks, by the way, were reclaimed from salt marshes. There is much more salt marsh—several hundred acres of it certainly—which could be reclaimed without great difficulty or expense. (If this were Holland, it would have been done long since.) This is because the rice grass, *Spartina townsendii*, has become established (no one knows how, though there are any number of legends about the original introduction) on many of the mudflats around the harbour. Spartina grass binds the mud, preventing erosion—in some places, though not here, it has been deliberately planted for this purpose—and, once established, it spreads with astonishing rapidity. There are several places around the shores of Poole Harbour where it is so well-established that it looks like meadow-land stretching out into the water, so green and apparently firm, the "fields" separated by reedy channels, that one is surprised not to see dairy cattle grazing them. One day, I suppose, the penny will drop and somebody will set about reclaiming these hundreds of acres. On economic grounds I feel sure that it ought to be done. I confess that I hope it will not be done during my lifetime. At present these marshes are a paradise for wading birds. Reclaim them, and the birds must go.

All this, of course, sets Poole apart from Bournemouth: indeed, from all the other seaside resorts that I know. But there is also something else, something impossible to pin down; an atmosphere, even in some measure a dignity, bestowed by age.

Poole is a very ancient town, and the harbour must have been, from the very earliest times, of great importance. (It would be so today were it not for the modern fetish for size.) This great sheltered stretch of shallow water must have been, for any boat big enough to cross the Channel, a most inviting place in which to lie up. There can be no doubt that the Celtic invaders used this harbour—as they did the smaller, equally sheltered, lagoon at Christchurch—long before the great earthworks were built on the hilltops of Dorset and Hampshire. The Romans certainly used it

4

Sailing in the river mouth at Mudeford

(there is evidence of a Roman settlement at Hamworthy) and, of course, for the Viking raiders this vast, sheltered stretch of water, with its secluded islands to confer safety from reprisal, was ideal. I think that nobody knows just how early there were settlements along the shores of this inland sea, but there can be no doubt at all that a town, and a flourishing one, was established on the present site—that is, on the eastern arm of the entrance to Holes Bay—in the eleventh century and well before the Conquest. That is ancient enough lineage.

By the thirteenth century the town and port had gained such importance that it was able to obtain, in 1248, a Charter of Liberties from the Lord of the Manor of Canford, William Longespee, the crusader whose monument is in Salisbury Cathedral. Under this charter it secured the right to hold its own courts and to appoint its own Port Reeve. Another charter, granted in 1371 by the Lord of the Manor, William Montacute, enacted that "our Port Reeve shall henceforth be styled Mayor". Poole has, therefore, elected its mayor for almost six hundred years. A further charter, granted in 1568 by Elizabeth I, made Poole "a County incorporate, separate and distinct from the County of Dorset". This charter also stated that the town should have a sheriff. Poole ceased to be a County Borough in 1888, to the great advantage of the County of Dorset, but it still has its sheriff, who at official functions carries a wand surmounted by a crown (signifying that he is the representative of the Monarch) and who, by ancient custom, entertains the Recorder at Quarter Sessions and takes his place on the Recorder's right during the sitting of the Court.

As one would expect of a seafaring town, Poole has its place, and a not inconsiderable one, in the history of piracy. Poole's pirate was Harry Page, the terror of the Channel and feared as far south as the Spanish coast, being known far and wide as "Arripay". He must have been a very formidable buccaneer, if it is true, as is related, that one expedition alone brought him one hundred and twenty prizes. At any rate, his depredations were sufficiently serious to bring retaliation. In 1405 a combined French and Spanish force under the command of Pero Nino landed on the Quay and pillaged the town. Piracy on a smaller scale continued for many years with Poole as base, but with the discovery of Newfoundland by the Cabots Poole turned to legitimate merchant trading. Poole men were among the first to settle in Newfoundland and there was thereafter a steady traffic between the new colony and the Dorset port. In the eighteenth and early part of the nineteenth century particularly some hundred ships sailed annually each spring with supplies for the Newfoundland fisherfolk and some Poole merchants amassed considerable fortunes. You can see the evidence of this in the fine town houses in Thames Street and West Street.

But, of course, not all the trade was legitimate. This has always been a smuggling coast. Not only were goods smuggled in, but many a man, wanted by the authorities, must have been conveyed to safer shores by Poole seamen. Monmouth was making his way to Poole when he was caught in a ditch a few miles north of the town. He must have known perfectly well that, if only he could reach the port, he had a very good chance of being smuggled to safety. The most famous of these escapees, Charles II after the Battle of Worcester, actually left from Shoreham in Sussex. But he left in a Poole coal brig, captained by a Poole man, which sailed regularly between the two ports. Poole had been a stronghold for Parliament against the King during the Civil War. Possibly Nicholas Tattersal, the brig's skipper was a Royalist: possibly the fee of £60 (a very considerable sum in those days) spoke louder than political loyalties. Charles did not forget. After the Restoration the little coal brig was taken round to London, anchored off Whitehall, and later, renamed *Royal Escape*, entered in the Royal Navy, Nicholas Tattersal being given a pension of £100 a year: a royal gesture indeed.

These Poole seamen, and particularly those on the wrong side of the law, were a tough and enterprising lot. One escapade, one of the boldest in smuggling history, does not deserve to be forgotten. In 1747 the revenue officers seized a valuable cargo of tea and put it in the Custom House on the quay for safe-keeping. It must have been a very valuable cargo—in other words, there must have been some very wealthy customers waiting to share it—for the smugglers were loath to lose it. They rallied reinforcements from among their "free trade" brethren and stormed the Custom House. They got the tea back and they got it away: that cargo was never recovered.

The Custom House, a charming example of Georgian design, still stands. Near the quayside, indeed, there are many buildings of historical and architectural interest. But the most notable of the ancient buildings in the town is Scaplen's Court, a quadrangular house of the late fourteenth century with fifteenth and sixteenth-century additions, which has had a very chequered history. It may well have been Poole's original Town Hall. In the seventeenth century it was an inn, known as "The George". In the eighteenth century it became the town house of John Scaplen, the Sheriff of Poole, and was then known as Scaplen's Court. Later it fell on evil days and was divided into tenements, degenerating into what was really a slum property. In 1929 it was rescued by the Society of Poole Men, who bought it and restored it (at very considerable expense), and then opened it to the public as "The Old Town House". The cost of running such a place was greater than could be met for long by a private body, no matter how public-spirited, and in 1931 it was taken over by the Poole Council. In 1950 it had to be closed, because it was considered structurally unsafe. Since then extensive restoration work has been carried out—this work has been done exceptionally well—and the building, which contains interesting exhibits of local life and history, but is not a museum in the strict sense, is now again open to the public.

Poole—that is, old Poole Town, the part on the small peninsula between Holes Bay and Parkstone Bay—is full of history, but the visitor has to search for it since it is, most of it, hidden away in odd corners. Comparatively few visitors bother to do so because, by the time they have reached the old town, they are frustrated, if not definitely short-tempered. Traffic is heavy, and matters are not improved by the level-crossings across the two main streets. But it is worthwhile persevering, for even if you are not interested in architecture or history, in yachts or small boats, even if you cannot derive amusement from the colourful eccentricities in dress beloved by sailing females, there are always the pubs of old Poole, filled with atmosphere and good manners and the tongues of many lands. And if you have a penchant for collecting, let me recommend the junk shops of old Poole. They are filled with treasures sold by foreign sailors to pay for a "night on the town".

Poole is, indeed, a fantastic and fascinating mixture of the very old and the ultra-modern, of the seafaring and the suburban. A town easy to fall in love with.

III

WEST OF AVON

WHERE, west of the Avon, to draw a boundary is, I have found, a matter of great difficulty so far as the scope of this book is concerned. The temptation is to go on and on: to include all the heathland as far west as Dorchester, as Ralph Wightman did in his excellent *The Wessex Heathland*. But this book is concerned, however loosely, with the New Forest. A boundary must be drawn.

If you look at the map showing the proposed amendment to local government boundaries—this was included in the Report of the New Forest Committee 1947, but no further action was taken; most unfortunately, in my opinion—you will see that county boundaries are ignored. A small portion of Dorset is included: quite a fair slice of Wiltshire. The northern boundary, shown on this map, follows the line of Wick Down westwards from Downton. That is natural enough and I follow it here, though, to the west of Wick Down, I have pushed my boundary a little further to the north, up to the line of Grim's Ditch. I do so only because this forms, as it did when it was built, a natural boundary.

But I find myself quite unable to agree with the western boundary as proposed by the New Forest Committee 1947 and shown on this map. As shown on the map this boundary seems to me to be quite arbitrary. There is a natural boundary on the north, but there is nothing natural at all about this western boundary; or, at least, the northern part of it, that part from Ashley Heath northwards.

Why include Ashley Heath and exclude Boveridge Heath? The stranger is quite unable to tell where the one ends and the other begins: for that matter, I have yet to find a local inhabitant sure on the point. The reason would seem to be that between Ashley Heath and Boveridge Heath, and southwards, the proposed boundary was drawn to follow the line of the county boundary between Dorset and Hampshire. But if that was so, there would seem to be no good reason for including Alderholt and Alderholt Common, which lie within the Dorset boundary, and excluding Cranborne Common, which adjoins and merges with Alderholt Common. And why include Damerham and Rockbourne, but exclude Martin? One gets the impression that somebody drew a straight line on a map without paying much attention to the character of the land. There may have been sound administrative reasons for this. Topographically, and from every other point of view, the proposed boundary here makes a nonsense.

I think that the county boundary south from Ashley Heath, following as it does the course of the Moors River for some distance, makes a natural and excellent boundary for the purpose of this book, just as it did in 1947 when it was proposed that all the land to the eastwards should be taken into the New Forest. But I cannot think it right to exclude Boveridge Heath and Cranborne Common. For the purpose of this book, therefore, the boundary will include both and will then run north-westwards, following pretty closely the line of the county boundary between Dorset and Hampshire, the line of the Bokerly Dyke, to the Blandford-Salisbury road and the border between Hampshire and Wiltshire; thus including Martin.

It may well be objected that this boundary is as arbitrary as that about which I have been complaining. And, of course, in large measure this is perfectly true. I, too, am drawing lines on a map. It is not, however, as arbitrary in that I have not attempted to separate commons which, even though they may bear different names, are, in fact, one. Nevertheless, looking at the map, there may seem to be no good reason why I should stop at the line I have drawn: no reason other than that I have got to stop somewhere.

I admit that, just looking at a map, that would, indeed, appear to be so. In fact, broadly speaking, this is a genuine boundary. It is true that, except in the far north-west corner, the nature of the country does not change all that much; and even there the change is not dramatic. At sight, there is not all that difference between Cranborne Chase and all the rest of it. After all, Cranborne Chase once included a great area of Hampshire and Wiltshire as well as Dorset—the original Chase was bounded on the north-east and south-west by the rivers Avon and Stour respectively, had an outer perimeter of about one hundred miles, and contained an area of some 700,000 acres—and, in character, was genuine forest land. Hardy described it as " a truly venerable tract of forest-land, one of the few remaining woodlands of England of undoubted primeval date, wherein Druidical mistletoe is still found on aged oaks, and where enormous yew trees, not planted by the hand of man, grow as they had grown when they were pollarded for bows". And that would not be a bad description of the New Forest.

It was used for the same purpose, too: namely, hunting. The word "chase" (a more modest title than that of "forest") indicated that the hunting rights over the district it comprised belonged to a subject. Normally it carried no rights of ownership of the property with it. Should a "chase" for any reason—and the usual one was mere "grab", the medieval form of nationalization—pass to the King, it at once became a "forest". Should it, at some later date, leave the King's charge, it immediately reverted to the more modest title. Cranborne Chase, though strictly a "chase" in the sporting sense, was also, however, the private property of the Earls of Gloucester. King John, before he came to the throne, married the heiress to that house and the property passed with her into his charge. At that time, of course, John was a subject and, therefore, the property remained a "chase". When he came to the throne—he divorced the lady soon after he did so, but took care to hang on to the property—it at once became a "forest" and subject to the full rigour of Norman Forest Law. Throughout the reign of King John there was no difference at all between Cranborne Forest and the New Forest: both were Royal Forests and administered as such. At John's death, however, the property reverted to the family of his first Queen and again became a "chase", no longer subject to the full rigour of the Forest Law. It remained with that family until the accession of Edward IV, when it again became a Royal Forest and continued to be such until the accession of James I, who granted it to the Earl of Salisbury. It then, of course, became a "chase" once more. Because of the original private ownership, because of the reversion to private ownership after the death of King John, because of the comparative lack of interest in deer hunting by later monarchs, because of the reversion to "chase" status with the accession of James I, the area (with the exception of the short period of King John's reign) really fell between two stools, was neither a "chase" in the full sense of the word nor a "forest" in the full sense of the word, Though final disafforestation was not achieved until 1830, the area, from the death of King John onwards, has always been more "chase" than "forest", has always been subject to the whims of private enterprise, its successes and follies, to a degree never achieved in the New Forest. And this has, of course, inevitably left its stamp. Although in character genuine forest land, it would be wholly wrong to include Cranborne Chase within the boundaries of this book. There is a difference: difficult to define, and certainly not apparent to the casual visitor, but nevertheless a real difference. Ralph Wightman, in his *The Wessex Heathland*, has put it thus:

The western part of Dorset was probably never under the same strict forest laws. To this day the difference remains. The Hampshire portion consists of settlements sitting on small patches of good land, the inhabitants of which have grazing and other rights on the open heath. The Dorset heath has no village within its true borders. All the farms, all the settlements are on the edge, or along the river valleys which cut across it. Any use which has ever been made of the heath, except for gravel workings and military exercises, has been from farms on its borders. There are very few heath men in Dorset in the sense that there are foresters in Hampshire. The old inhabitants of Burley and Bramshaw are Forest men. They are enclosed by the Forest. The very names of the Dorset heaths show that they are not a real part of the villages. Piddletown, Bere Regis, Wool, Moreton and Canford all have heaths, but the villages are on kindlier, more tractable soil. The New Forest parishes are part of this strange, isolated land. The inhabitants live, to a large extent, from the Yetene Heath. In Dorset the villages are like little ports on the edge of the barren, bitter sea. It is a fair analogy to think of the dwellers in the New Forest as living on small islands surrounded by the heath, while the Dorset men are on the mainland. Both use the heath and live from it, but to the Forester it is more important.

Ralph Wightman was born and brought up, and has spent his life-time, on the Dorset heath, or rather, in one of the little ports on the edge of it. But he has also had close connections with the New Forest since childhood. He knows instinctively what cannot, from its very nature, be apparent to the casual visitor. His is a true, a penetrating, analysis of the difference.

My boundary, though apparently an arbitrary line drawn on the map, does, in fact, delineate that difference; does mark the frontier between the life of "the small islands surrounded by the heath" and the life of the mainland. Of course, this frontier is not so well-defined north-westwards from Ashley Heath to the Wiltshire border as it is by the Moors River southwards from Ashley Heath. Of course, there is, under the pressures of modern life, some blurring here and there. Nevertheless, even though all this area was once part of Cranborne Chase, my line does define fairly accurately the demarcation between the "chase" influence and the "forest" influence.

The area of land south of Ashley Heath, a rough triangle with West Moors at its apex, has fallen altogether under the influence of the two large towns on the coast. The northern suburbs of Poole, interspersed with heathland, reach up to the Stour, almost to the confines of Wimborne Minster. Beyond the Stour is Ferndown and beyond Ferndown, northwards, West Moors. Both Ferndown and West Moors—and I suppose that this might also now be said of Verwood, even further to the north—may properly be described as suburbs of Bournemouth and Poole, and so, I suppose, may all the land south of Ashley Heath, lying be-tween the Moors River and the outskirts of Bournemouth proper.

This triangle of country has altered greatly in my lifetime: particularly since the war. Essentially it is a stretch of low-lying sour land, a land of pines and gorse scrub: typical low-lying heath. When I was a boy it was virtually uninhabited for the simple reason that nobody could make a living out of it. There were a few small-holdings and that was about all. I do not recall that there was even a place called Ferndown then. Today, Ferndown is wealthy and "posh" with a first-class hotel and a magnificent golf course. It really is wonderful what can be done with barren heathland when there is sufficient money available. Consider the magnificent golf courses in the Bournemouth-Poole area with their perfect green and mown fairways, all won from the desolate heath, and remember that this could, undoubtedly, also be done agriculturally, if there was sufficient money available. (But cows, of course, do not pay the same sort of subscription as golfers!) And if there is not sufficient money. . . .

Between the wars, encouraged presumably by the cheapness of the land and the proximity of Bournemouth, a lot of ex-service men put their gratuities into buying small plots of land and setting-up as market-gardeners or poultry farmers: and went bankrupt. Their fate did not discourage others, most of whom went the same way. And it happened again after the last war. Today very few survive.

But today there are any number of bungalows and small brick villas, and a few of the old cobb-and-thatch cottages, lining the lanes all through this stretch of heathland. The area is now much sought after residentially, has become an estate agent's paradise. And some of the gardens are beautiful. But gardening—yes, even gardening—on this soil is not easy. Leave one for a few months and the heath is back, the hungry sand supreme.

From the southern boundary of Ashley Heath northwards the contrast is quite startling. Again we have a roughly triangular area, with its base on the Avon and Martin at its apex, low-lying sour heathland, similar in every way to the land immediately to the south. In every way, that is, except population. North of the sprawl of St. Leonards and St. Ives on either side of the A31— an indeterminate villadom which might be a suburb of Ringwood were Ringwood large enough to support such a thing) or an off-shoot of Bournemouth's suburban spread, but which seems to have grown up for no reason other than the presence of the trunk road—the soil is the same, as obviously inhospitable but no more so. Yet habitation virtually ceases. There is a small farm or two, widely separated, little islands in the barren heath, but there is no settlement between Ashley and Alderholt, neither of which is really more than a hamlet. So the land, in this southern corner of the triangle, is given up to its proper purpose, which is the growing of timber. Ashley Heath, Boveridge Heath, New Heath, Plumley Heath—and no man can tell you with certainty where the one ends and the next begins—form together one great woodland, and there is more land on the immediate confines of this woodland which could usefully be planted. None of this, other than the few patches which are already cultivated, will ever make farm land. It is too far from a good shopping centre, too isolated, communications too bad (it is virtually laneless), ever to become a retirement centre. But it could grow more trees. The recommendation of the 1947 Committee that this area—or most of it, for the Committee was prepared to split the woodland in two (and pretty well down the middle at that) for some reason which it did not make plain and which I have never been able to understand—be included within the New Forest for administrative purposes was undoubtedly sound.

In the hey-day of Cranborne Chase, Alderholt, which lies just within the Dorset border and at the northern limit of the area I have been discussing, was a place of some importance. It was the seat of the "gentleman-ranger" who was in charge of Alderholt Walk—a "walk" being an area of woodland specially planted and preserved for the deer—and so was the administrative centre for this part of the Chase. I suppose that it must be because of this that Alderholt is given such prominence on the Ordnance Survey map, which is rather misleading because Alderholt is not today important in any way at all. It is a pleasant, quiet little village with an undistinguished church and a very ancient history. Not that anything important enough to achieve the history books—even the local history books, which is saying a great deal!—has ever happened at Alderholt, but the history is ancient enough, for Bronze Age man lived here and there are a number of tumuli, and at least one barrow, in the neighbourhood.

Alderholt, indeed, is by way of being a sort of frontier village. From here, northwards and north-westwards, the nature of the country begins to change. Southwards, and all the way to the coast, it has been low-lying, rarely attaining a height of even 100 feet above sea-level: flat, sour heathland, inhospitable and hungry. Until the end of the first World War all this land from Alderholt to the coast, west of the narrow valley of the Avon, was virtually deserted. There were a few, very few, isolated "island" farms whose owners scratched a scanty living from the hungry heath: and that was all. And that has been the pattern all through the ages. I believe that I am correct in saying that from the immediate neighbourhood of Alderholt all the way to the immediate neighbourhood of Hengistbury Head you will not find a single tumulus. Bronze Age man, Iron Age man, Roman, Saxon, Norman, all also found this land too inhospitable. But from Alderholt northwards there are more and more signs of the presence of Bronze Age man, more and more signs of early settlement. It is inescapable that Alderholt was, in those days, an outpost, the frontier post so to speak, on the edge of the sour flatlands.

Except for the southerly portion, that part lying seawards of the A31 which has come under the influence of the Bournemouth conurbation, the picture is not really so very different today. As I have said, there is no settlement, and scarcely a farm, between Ashley and Alderholt. But northwards of Alderholt the ground begins to rise, becomes undulating, the ridges rarely of any height to begin with but sometimes surprisingly steep, and climbs steadily until towards the border heights approaching 400 feet are achieved and genuine heathland gives way to downland. And with the change in the pattern of country comes a change in the pattern and frequency of settlement. Not that this is a thickly populated countryside. Far from it: there are only four villages and they are small. But it is a well populated countryside, the farms becoming more and more frequent, and larger, as one leaves Alderholt behind. This has been a settled, a well populated, countryside for a very long time.

Let us consider the villages first. Damerham, the village nearest to Alderholt, lies in the narrow valley of the Allen River. Here there is evidence of long settlement in the fine church, which stands to the south-west of, and a little apart from, the village itself. The tower, which was never finished, is Norman with later buttresses and the nave, the north arcade, and the chancel are also Norman. At one time the chancel had chapels on either side and the blocked arcades of these still remain. One gets the impression that the original Norman structure was intended to be something much larger than a church for a small hamlet (which Damerham must have been at the time the building was started), but if that was so, then the history has been lost. Over the south doorway there is a Norman tympanum. This was found built into the vicarage and was placed in its present position in 1920. It shows St. George at the battle of Antioch in 1098, depicting the legend that the saint was seen by the Crusaders at the head of a large army, a sight which so encouraged the small force led by Godfrey de Bouillon that it gained a resounding victory over the Saracens. The panelled roofs of the nave, the chancel and the porch are good fifteenth-century work, and the church contains some real treasures; among them a beautiful Italian Renaissance altar cross dated 1556. To the south-east of the church there is a stone, once used as a cheese press, which has an incised cross and is said to be of Celtic origin. There is no doubt about the cheese press story, but, as one might expect, the experts do not agree about the Celtic origin. It does, however, seem rather more likely than not.

If you leave Damerham by the Martin road and take the first turning to the right, you climb a little hill—at the top you are only 200 feet above sea level—and then drop down to the narrow valley of the Bourne, a tiny stream which joins the Allen just before the latter joins the Avon at Fordingbridge, and so to the village of Rockbourne. Rockbourne is just one long street with pretty cottages lining the little stream, one of the pleasantest villages in all Hampshire. The church has been much restored, but the original building was an early twelfth-century cruciform structure and of this the archway into the north transept, which is now the vestry, remains. Later there may have been a monastic foundation here. To the north of the church are the extensive remains of what was once the Elizabethan manor house and here is a farm with some very intriguing buildings. Among them is a barn, which is of thirteenth-century date and was once almost certainly a chapel.

To get to Martin it is better to return along the Damerham road and to take the lane which runs up the Allen valley, the downs arising on either hand in broad, open, gentle sweeps. Martin lies at the head of the valley, here wide enough to be called a vale. Most English villages have a definite beginning and end, but not Martin. Somehow I am always surprised when I enter the village and as surprised when I find that I have left it, so much is it part of its background, so anonymously does it emerge from the downland and fade back into it. It is not the sort of place and is not in the sort of situation, open and windswept (Damerham and Rockbourne are both sheltered), where you would expect to find an ancient church. Yet here is a church of exceptional interest. The original building, of which there now remains only the blocked north doorway with its plain tympanum, was aisleless Norman. This original building has been greatly enlarged at different periods. The Decorated chancel was added in the fourteenth century and the south transept a little later in the same century. The Perpendicular north transept was added in the fifteenth century and the north chapel in the sixteenth. The lower portion of the tower is Early English, the belfry Perpendicular, and the parapet and the spire are dated 1787. Well, you may say, there is surely nothing exceptional in that. And, of course, that is true: there are any number of churches up and down the length and breadth of England with a similar architectural history. Nevertheless, Martin Church is exceptional. For I think that you will find that in all other cases in which a parish church has been enlarged or beautified there has been wealth in the immediate neighbourhood; a rich religious foundation or a rich landowner who, though building to the glory of God, was determined at the same time to glorify his own name and that of his family. That was not the case here. Martin has never been a big village—the present population, numbering but a few hundred, is certainly the largest in all its long history—has never been the seat of a great landowning family, has never enjoyed the patronage of a rich and generous religious foundation. Yet, here, in this humble village, there has been church building all through the ages, from the late eleventh (or very early twelfth) century onwards, the church growing steadily (and quite unnecessarily) larger and larger and, with the addition of the parapet and the spire, more imposing. Why? And who paid for it all, all through the centuries? There is no local stone, which means there were no local craftsmen: stone, craftsmen, everything, had to be brought in. It must have been an expensive exercise at the best of times: a positively astonishing one for a little village whose population could only have been employed in local agriculture, always the most poorly paid of English industries.

Whitsbury, the last of the four villages, is best approached from Fordingbridge: it is all too easy to lose your way otherwise. Lying in a wooded combe in lovely surroundings, Whitsbury has almost certainly been a settlement for as long as the other three: but here there is no architectural evidence of age. But, by name at least (none is much visited), Whitsbury is certainly by far the most widely known of the four. For here is the stud belonging to William Hill and here has been bred many a famous racehorse, and here, too, is the training establishment of Sir Gordon Richards. This little Hampshire village has, indeed, a national fame. We are a nation of gamblers.

Now let us return to Martin and climb the down to the Bokerly Dyke. It is a gentle climb and the height at the top is only 300 feet above sea-level. But from here you look down on the wastes of the New Forest, dun-coloured in the sunlight, dark and somehow rather forbidding in the rain. Six long-lived cultures have left their signatures on this north-western area beyond Alderholt, and particularly on the high ground that runs from Martin Down eastwards to Whitsbury and Breamore Down. But you must walk the down paths and tracks if you would see them. The exploration of this area of comparatively high ground provides a series of most rewarding walks; none, from a car left on one of the lanes, of any great distance. You will need the Ordnance Survey One-inch Map and you will need time: perhaps a fortnight, so constantly will you find yourself diverted off to the right hand and the left as you go, if you wish to do it thoroughly.

West Bournemouth

The oldest of these cultures is the Neolithic (New Stone Age, *circa* 2500–1900 B.C.), whose signature here is the Long Barrow. The Long Barrow is a burial mound, which may be several hundred feet in length and which is always broader and higher at one end than at the other. The larger end, by the way, usually points to the east. It is supposed that originally all these Long Barrows had containing walls of timber, but now they appear just as long turf-grown mounds of chalk. Here on Martin Down, just behind the Bokerly Dyke (and actually a few yards over my boundary; but I think it allowable to digress that much), there is a group of three of them. On the other side of the vale, behind Martin, on the edge of Toyd Down, a mile or so from the Allen River, are two more; Knap Barrow and Grans Barrow. If you then follow the track from Grans Barrow—it is clearly shown on the Ordnance Survey One-inch Map of the New Forest—cross the Rockborne lane and continue to the top of the hill, you will come to the curiously named Duck's Nest, which is a Long Barrow in the middle of nowhere with a priest-like yew rising from the undergrowth that covers the mound. If you have left your car at the point where the track from Grans Barrow crosses the Rockbourne lane, it is then a simple matter to return to it from the Duck's Nest and to follow the lane northwards to Little Toyd Down where there is a another group of Long Barrows, two on your left hand, two on your right, just short of Grim's Ditch. There are two more Long Barrows on Breamore Down, close by the Miz-Maze (to which we will come later), one of which is known as the Giant's Grave.

The Neolithic Age was succeeded by the Bronze Age, which the specialists divide into three periods: early, middle, and late. The non-specialist will be wise to eschew such niceties. It is sufficient for him to know that the stone circle (Stonehenge, for example) and the stone row belong to the earliest period of the Bronze Age and that the Round Barrow is characteristic of the Bronze Age (*circa* 1900–450 B.C.) as a whole. There is no stone circle nor stone row in the area we are exploring, but there are plenty of Round Barrows.

Round Barrows are usually marked on the maps as "tumuli",

5

A cricket match at Swan Green near Lyndhurst

a generic term for any ancient burial mound other than a Long
Barrow. There are said to be about forty thousand Round
Barrows still standing in England alone; and, of course, a great
many have been levelled in the interests of agricultural development and particularly since the advent of the tractor. Considering
the numbers and the long period of years through which this form
of burial flourished—and it extended beyond the Bronze Age—
one would expect to find a considerable "architectural" variation
in the Round Barrow. And such, indeed, is the case. They vary in
construction, and very greatly in size; from as little as four to five
yards to as much as fifty to sixty yards in diameter and in height
from as little as a foot to as much as twenty feet. The earliest form
is known as the Bowl Barrow, recognizable by its pudding-shaped
mound immediately encircled by a ditch. Later came the Bell
Barrow, recognizable by the wide, level, "berm" between the
edge of the mound and the encircling ditch, which gives to the
whole the silhouette of a flanged bell, and the Disk Barrow, in
which there is a low bank on the outer rim of the encircling ditch
and in which the mound is always very low. These are the three
main types of Round Barrow: there are others, but their identification is not easy for the non-expert. Though the Bowl Barrow is
the earliest form it must not be thought that it was wholly superseded by the advent of the Bell Barrow and the Disk Barrow.
That was not the case. The Bowl Barrow continued to be built
throughout the period of the Bronze Age and well beyond it.
Indeed, there is some evidence that both the Romans and the
Saxons used this form of burial mound occasionally, though they
do not appear to have used the more advanced types of Round
Barrow.

About 450 B.C. the Bronze Age gave way to the Iron Age, which
lasted until the Roman Conquest in A.D. 43. If the Round Barrow,
even more than the stone circle and the stone row, is the unmistakable signature of the Bronze Age, the Hill-Fort is the unmistakable
signature of the Iron Age. Grahame Clark, in his *Prehistoric
England*, has this to say of the hill-fort:

Hill-Forts are at once among the most impressive and informative of our prehistoric antiquities. They impress by their mere size, by the height of their ramparts, by the depth of their ditches, by the extent of the areas they enclose, and frequently by their commanding position. The disproportion between their immensity and the relatively low stage of development attained by the communities responsible for them shows that in their day they must have fulfilled a need of overwhelming importance. . . . Their economic and social significance is still debated, but their primary purpose as defensive works is not to be doubted.

Within the area we are exploring there are two, Damerham Knoll and Whitsbury Castle Ditches, of these hill-top earthworks. A third, Clearbury Ring, four miles north of Whitsbury, is just outside our boundary, but should be visited at the same time because it provides a marked contrast with the other two and the three together pose so clearly the problem outlined in the last sentence of that quotation from Grahame Clark.

Clearbury Ring is placed in a strong position on an isolated hill between the Ebble and the Avon. It is a single-ramparted enclosure (now completely filled with beech trees and Scots pine) and it is connected with Whitsbury by a branch of the linear earthwork (a bank and ditch) known as Grim's Ditch, the main arm of which follows a somewhat zig-zag course due westwards across Little Toyd Down. It is evident from its very nature that Grim's Ditch could not have been a defensive work and one can only suppose that it was built to define a boundary; perhaps a tribal boundary. You have but to look at Clearbury Ring in its commanding position to realize that it must have been built primarily for defensive purposes.

Then why was it necessary to build another, very much larger and infinitely stronger, hill-top earthwork only four miles away? Whitsbury Castle Ditches, also in a commanding position, is not rectangular but oval (the shape, of course, is dictated by the lie of the ground) and has triple ramparts of immense strength. This was a major construction. True, it does not compare for size with Maiden Castle or with a number of other southern hill-forts. Nevertheless, this was a major fortification: obviously the centre, the headquarters, of all this area.

That being so—and I do not think that it can be questioned—
what could have been the necessity for the undistinguished (now
tree-grown) earthwork on Damerham Knoll, a mere mile and a
half to the south-west? This, by comparison with Clearbury Ring
and Whitsbury Castle Ditches, is tiny, has not a particularly commanding position, and has not got a very forbidding rampart. By
comparison with the other two it is a primitive construction and
does not really give (as they do) the impression of being a fortified
position. Certainly it would have been impossible to defend in the
face of anything like a determined attack.

Now, the Bronze Age for almost the whole of its long, long life
—at least here, in the south of England—was an age of peace. The
evidence for this is Stonehenge. Stonehenge was carefully planned
and took a very long time to complete; a matter of five hundred
years or more. (R. J. C. Atkinson has suggested the period 1900–
1400 B.C. for the completion of the whole.) Generation after
generation of builders could have worked only in times of settled
peace. And there is the further evidence of the stones that were
used. It has been proved beyond all doubt, by petrological analysis, that the blue stones, each weighing upwards of four tons, were
brought from the Prescelly Mountains in Pembrokeshire. Such
huge stones could not have been transported all the way from
south Wales (transport in Bronze Age Britain must have been
exceptionally well-organized) had not the country (all the country, all the way from Wiltshire to Pembrokeshire, as well as the
seas around the coasts, for these great stones were almost certainly
water-borne) enjoyed peace, a sure and settled peace under assured
and unquestioned central authority.

That peace ended with the invasions of the Iron Age Celts. The
Celts did not, of course, wipe out the Bronze Age inhabitants.
They imposed their authority upon them, as is the way of conquerors. To begin with the Celtic invaders would not have been
very strong in numbers, though greatly superior in weapons, and
they would have needed fortified camps not only for their own
protection in hostile country, but also as centres from which they
could exercise their authority. (The Normans built their castles
for precisely the same reason.) One would expect, therefore, the

first hill-forts to be thrown up in a bit of a hurry; to be pretty primitive in construction, just a single rampart.

On this reasoning, the enclosure on Damerham Knoll, the most primitive of the three we are discussing, would have been the first in this area. I do not believe that it was. The site is not sufficiently commanding. I think that the first Iron Age hill-fort hereabouts was at Clearbury. Here is a most commanding position and here is the single rampart, a pretty formidable one, that one would expect of a fortification designed in a hurry. Granted the great superiority in weapon power, which we know the Celts possessed, this was a virtually impregnable position.

Why, then, the great fort at Whitsbury? Why, with Clearbury already in existence, bother to build this great fort with its triple ramparts? Are we to suppose that the country was not truly conquered, that Clearbury was not strong enough, was always in danger of being over-run? There is no evidence to suggest that the Celts had all that trouble in putting down the Bronze Age people. On the contrary, all the evidence suggests that the first Celtic invaders experienced little difficulty in imposing their authority on a peacable people. But there were waves of Celtic invaders, each as land hungry as the one before. They had to find living-room and they could do so only by coming to terms with, or subjecting, those already in occupation. I think that this is what happened here. I think that the first Iron Age settlers here, the builders of Clearbury, were over-run by a later and more powerful group, and that this second group then took care to see to it that the same thing did not happen to them. Hence the larger, infinitely stronger, earthwork at Whitsbury.

What, then, of the small earthwork on Damerham Knoll? This is by far the most primitive of the three, but I believe that it was the last to be built: that it was not built until long after the completion of the great fort at Whitsbury: that it was not built until the boundaries (perhaps those of a small principality, perhaps those of a great estate) had been delineated by the two arms of Grim's Ditch: in fact, that it was not built until all this area was settled and under firm control. What was its purpose? Well, it is evident that it was never intended to be a defensive work against outside attack. It was, I believe, a livestock corral. It must be remembered that the Celts, in addition to being a most warlike people, were good farmers and pastoralists, good sheep farmers, keepers of cattle and pigs. There is on Rockbourne Down (from the top of which, incidentally, you can see on a clear day all the way from Inkpen Beacon on the Berkshire-Hampshire border to the gap of Corfe Castle: a most satisfying view) just to the north of Damerham Knoll the site of an Iron Age farm; and it is surely significant that, three miles or so to the south-west, there is the site of another Iron Age farm and close by, on Pembury Knoll, just such another small enclosure.

Of Roman occupation there are but few signs. On Rockbourne Down there is an extensive Romano-British enclosure and another very similar one, which is known as Soldier's Ring, lies to the south-west over the Allen River. Both are definitely of Roman date and both are believed to be Roman pastoral corrals. No Roman villa has been found in the area and this has led to the suggestion that this land formed part of an Imperial estate, on which the farmers worked directly for the central administration, helping towards the up-keep of the army and so on, and not for themselves.

The one big Roman work in the area is the Bokerly Dyke, which forms our boundary. Seen from the Blandford–Salisbury road this earthwork does not appear very impressive. But, if you look at it from its eastern end, as it swings up over Tidpit Down and Pentridge Hill to Martin Down and the Blandford–Salisbury road, it appears, even today, as a pretty formidable barrier. And that was exactly what it was intended to be. Unlike the much older Grim's Ditch, this was not built to mark a boundary. This was a defensive work. As seen today, it may appear a rather ineffective one, since at each end it just peters out, giving the impression that it could easily be out-flanked. We may be sure that the Romans were not so foolish as that. When this earthwork was built the country at either end of it must have been considered impassable; and was, presumably, impenetrable forest. The Bokerly Dyke is late Roman, dating from the first half of the fourth century. This was the time of the great Pictish raids, which reached their peak in A.D. 367, and it gives some idea of the panic those raids must have caused for such a barrier as this to be built so far south.

Let us now return to our northern boundary, Grim's Ditch, where it runs across Little Toyd Down. If you walk eastwards along the Ditch here, you will come to Great Yews. There are many fine and ancient yews in Britain, most of them in church-yards, but Great Yews Wood is surely the most venerable and majestic grove that survives throughout England.

There is something cathedral-like, shrine-like, about Great Yews Wood. Even at high noon on a sunny day you are, in the fastness of the wood, in a twilight, so embracing is the shade. None of the trees is very high—I do not know how high: maybe, forty to fifty feet is the maximum—and they are not crowded together, but astonishingly regularly spaced out, but the girth of some of their boles is immense and the wide spread of their branches forms a patterned canopy of shade. The illusion of a cathedral is enhanced by the structure of the trunks. Some of them rise in one piece, great columns reaching upwards. Some are split into a number of separate trunks, resembling the clustered shafts which are such a feature of many of our cathedrals. Here, one is tempted to think, is "Early English" at its earliest. But then there are trunks so split and twisted that they resemble knots of writhing serpents: and now one might be in an oriental temple. I have spoken of the twilight of Great Yews Wood. Twilight it is, but a colourful twilight, for the great boles have a terra-cotta glow: a twilight shot with the muted colours of old stained glass at the hour before the candles are lit. In Great Yews Wood it is easy to understand why the yew was venerated by the Druids, why throughout our history it has played such a supreme part in the symbolism of death.

From Great Yews Wood a track runs south-eastwards over the Down, a track whose course is signposted with small yews and a profusion of wild flowers, to the other branch of Grim's Ditch. When you reach the Ditch, turn right and walk along it, south westwards, until you come to another track on your left-hand. Follow this over Breamore Down, and there is the Miz-Maze.

(This is not as long a walk as it sounds; barely a couple of miles.)
Whatever you do, visit the Miz-Maze.

As we see it today the Miz-Maze is a series of eleven elliptic
circles surrounding a central cone of turf some two feet high. Its
length, measured from the central cone to the furthest circum-
ference is seventeen yards and the outermost rim covers an area of
twenty-one yards. The whole is surrounded by a hedge of yew
about eight feet high—every time I have been I have found this
hedge trimmed—and this whole is set in the midst of a tangled
wood, in which some Round Barrows lie hidden in the undergrowth, on a windswept hill in one of the loneliest regions you
can find anywhere in the south of England. A few yards away to
the south-west, just beyond the edge of the wood, is the Long
Barrow known as The Giant's Grave. Beyond that, nothing:
nothing at all. It really is a most astonishing place.

There are said to be seven of these labyrinths existing in
England—these seven do not, of course, include any of the Tudor
mazes, like that at Hampton Court, which are purely ornamental
and which were designed for idle enjoyment: "quaint mazes on
the wanton green", as Shakespeare has it—but I know personally
only two others. One—in which the plan is square, not circular
like the Miz-Maze—is on St Catherine's Hill, a prehistoric site
with an Iron Age earthwork, near Winchester. The other, to
which I was taken by the late H. J. Massingham, is at Troy Farm
near Somerton, a small and isolated Oxfordshire village. I do not
know that Troy Farm itself is a prehistoric site, but the area in
which it is situated is rich in prehistoric remains. Some four miles
to the north, as the crow flies, is Rainsbarrow Camp, an Iron Age
earthwork: some two miles to the south, as the crow flies, is Aves
Ditch, a tribal boundary like Grim's Ditch: to the west is another
Iron Age earthwork above Nether Worton, and the Enstone
dolmen, and, but a little further on, the Rollright Stones.

By far the most perfect and detailed of these three mazes—and,
by general agreement, of all the seven—is the Miz-Maze. Yet we
know nothing about it. We do not know who made it: we do not
know its date. It is commonly presumed to be medieval. It may
well be. But it may well be very, very much older. Indeed, I think

that, in conception at least, it must be. I find it difficult to believe that its situation, as is also the case with the other two mazes I have mentioned, in an area rich in prehistoric remains can be mere coincidence.

But what was its purpose? Again, we do not know. It is believed to be a kind of chart, scored in the turf, of the convolutions of sin and error. If you patiently follow the windings of the causeways between the grooves of chalk, you will in the end win to the central cone, to Paradise. There is no straight and narrow path to Heaven, but only the circuitous one of stumbling and error.

It may well be that this is the correct interpretation. If it is, then the Miz-Maze is certainly medieval. But, if this is the correct interpretation, a lot of pertinent questions are left unanswered. Why was it made in this lonely spot, far from anywhere? Why have we no record of its construction? If it is medieval, if it had the religious significance accorded to it by modern interpretation, then it would surely have been visited by pilgrims, by repentant sinners, by somebody; and its use would surely have been recorded somewhere. But the fact is that we have no record of the Miz-Maze, no record of any of the seven mazes: not one medieval word. It is very odd indeed.

Myself, I have no doubt whatsoever of the religious significance of the Miz-Maze. I am quite sure that this was a sacred site. But I question the medieval origin. I question the modern interpretation: every word of it. I feel quite sure that this was a sacred site in prehistoric, in pagan times, and I think that it was one of those places whose traditional sanctity was maintained from paganism to Christianity. But I also feel sure that it was not one of those sacred pagan sites which was adopted by official Christianity. Had it been there would, surely, have been some record in the monkish chronicles. No, I think that this was a sacred site, a dedicated place, the folk-memory of which lingered on, which the peasantry visited "unbeknownst" and for a purpose of which they knew full well their religious mentors would not approve. I believe that for centuries young men and maidens came here, came up from Breamore and the other valley villages, in the dark, to walk the circuitous paths hand-in-hand, to sanctify upon the central cone at sunrise a rite far, far older than Christianity.

As they came up in the dark from Breamore, let us go down in the daylight: down to the Avon where we began this journey. On the further bank lies the New Forest proper.

IV

THE NEW FOREST: BACKGROUND

To understand anything of the New Forest as it is today, it is necessary to understand something of its history. It is a very long story, of course: but it is a not unentertaining one and, fortunately, there is no need to go all the way back to the beginning.

We need not bother about Stone Age man. There is no Long Barrow between the Avon and Southampton Water, no evidence of anything that could properly be called settlement. The Bronze Age is but little better represented. There are Round Barrows of various types, about 130 in all, the majority in the south of the region, but there is nothing to suggest that the Bronze Age people were settled here in any numbers. Nor is there evidence of settlement by Iron Age Celts on any scale. There is a hill-fort just west of Godshill Inclosure, but this properly belongs to the Avon valley and not to the Forest, and there is a triple-ramparted earthwork at Buckland Rings near Lymington. This is a plateau site and would not have been easy to defend. It certainly does not suggest that there was any large settlement in the area. Nor is there any evidence of Roman settlement: no Roman villa has been found within the area. There may have been a minor port, now eroded by the sea, near Lepe, for a Roman road runs from the coast there northwards to Dibden. Part of another Roman road is traceable near Stoney Cross. Evidence of Romano-British potteries has been found at a number of places within the Forest, but no evidence of permanent settlement. It would seem that the potters were itinerants, staying only a short time in each place.

The Saxon period is just as blank archaeologically. There is absolutely nothing to suggest that they settled the Forest, but it is at this time that the region is first mentioned in recorded history. According to the *Anglo-Saxon* Chronicle, which is a late ninth-century work based on earlier records, Cerdic and Cynric landed at Cerdices ora (which may have been Ower, at the entrance to Southampton Water) and fought with the Welsh. These two were the founders of the Royal House of Wessex, the family of which Alfred the Great was a member. They are interesting characters, these two, for, though they led the West Saxons to a kingdom, their names are not Saxon. The names are Welsh and the names of all their immediate descendants are Welsh: and the Welsh are the same people as the Britons, who were conquered by the Romans and who, after the Romans had left, came back to enjoy a brief reign before the coming in force of the Saxons. There can be no mistake about these names. These are the names of Welshmen; that is to say, of Britons. All the chroniclers agree about them, and all the chroniclers whenever they use Saxon names (Hengist and Horsa, for example) get them right. There is no possibility of confusion here. We can be quite sure that when the chroniclers tell us that Cadwalla—and you could not want a more Welsh name than that!—reconquered the Isle of Wight, which was held by South Saxons, and that he was the direct descendant of Cerdic, then they are right. So what were these two, Cerdic and Cynric, doing in this galley, leading an army of West Saxons? There is a pleasant little problem here; and, of course, no one knows the answer. Myself, I think that the answer must be that Cerdic and Cynric were the sons of a Saxon father and a Welsh (British) mother, that the mother was the stronger character of the two, that she gave her children British names and brought them up with British ways of thought, educating them, so far as she could, in the British culture. I think that the marked success of the Kingdom of Wessex can best be explained thus: that, from its inception, it was not entirely alien to the native way of life and thought. Be that as it may: there is no evidence that Cerdic and Cynric, nor after them Cadwalla, and their people settled in the New Forest. They passed through to the high and open chalk lands beyond.

As Dr Gordon J. Copley, in his contribution to the symposium, *The New Forest*, has said:

At no time, ancient, medieval or modern, has the New Forest provided a livelihood for a large population. Around its borders, along the coast, in the Avon valley and beside Southampton Water, there has probably been a sparse population almost since man first entered the region about half a million years ago, but the interior lands in most ages have had little to offer him. Infertile heathland and heavily forested lowland, interspersed with areas of bog, are attractive only to hunters and the keepers of swine or cattle, and these were almost the only inhabitants until modern times.

What then are we to make of the history book account of the making of the New Forest? You will know it well enough. William the Conqueror, we are told, laid waste the land to make his "New Forest". We have all read that he was so passionately fond of hunting that, to satisfy his passion, he laid waste a great area of fertile Hampshire, driving out the inhabitants, demolishing churches and manors and whole villages, destroying everything, to make room for more and more deer. We all know; because it is all in the history books. And the history books derive their authority from the old chronicles: so the history books must speak truth.

Well, let us take a brief glance at the old chronicles. It is an enlightening, and entertaining, exercise.

The earliest of these chroniclers is William Gemeticensis, who was a Norman. Writing shortly after the death of William Rufus in 1100, he says: "many, however, say, *ferunt autem multi*, that the deaths of Rufus and his brother were a judgement from heaven, because their father had destroyed many villages and churches in enlarging the New Forest". Now, it is evident from this that Gemeticensis is not concerned with the making of the New Forest—he is not commenting upon that at all—but with the mysterious death of William Rufus. He does not say that the Conqueror did, in fact, destroy "many villages and churches". What he is reporting is the gossip of a superstitious and fearful people, who had no cause to love the Normans. The whole thing is as vague as one would expect it to be. Superstition and rumour are never exact.

That honest report of the whispered gossip of a conquered people was to be used, and embellished, again and again. It is fascinating to note how, the further from the event the chronicler, the more definite and precise does the information become. Henry of Huntingdon, writing some twenty-five years after Gemeticensis, reports the gossip as fact: "He ordered the churches and villages to be destroyed and the people to be driven out." Here, there is no report of rumour, of superstitious gossip: this is a simple statement of fact. William of Malmesbury, writing at about the same time and using the same source, namely Gemeticensis, is more precise. He says that the Conqueror destroyed churches and villages "for more than thirty miles". But he is not content with that. He also says that the people were "exterminated"; not merely driven out. The Winchester chronicle adds a further embellishment, saying that "for the space of thirty miles, the whole country, which was fruitful to a high degree, was laid waste". Florence of Worcester, while not committing himself to figures, gives the same impression of fertility, saying that the land was "full of the habitations of men and thick-set with churches" before the Conqueror laid hands on it.

A little later, the immediate impact of the Conquest forgotten, the fear of savage retribution less, the chroniclers (all of whom, it must be remembered, were monks) become bolder in the use of figures; all of them sufficiently vague to be impressive, all of them designed to enhance the position of the Church. Oderic tells us that "more than sixty parishes" were destroyed: Knighton that "to make room for his beasts of chase, he destroyed twenty-two churches, some say fifty-two, together with villages, chapels, and private houses, and formed the New Forest, which he called his garden". The sober chronicler has become the unashamed political propagandist!

Finally, we have Walter Mapes, Archdeacon of Oxford under Henry II, who, writing more than a century after the event, at a time when the Norman conquerors were beginning to lose their separate identity and at a time when the power of the Church almost rivalled that of the King, tells us that "the Conqueror took away much land from God and men, and converted it to the use of wild beasts and the sport of his dogs; for which he demolished thirty-six churches and exterminated the inhabitants". Thirty-six churches: you could not wish for more precise information. The superstitious gossip occasioned by the mysterious death of William Rufus and so faithfully recorded for what it was by William Gemeticensis, the superstitious gossip which was to make useful political propaganda for the Church in the hands of some later chroniclers, has become history, made respectable by Walter Mapes. His account was accepted without question—after all, he was an archdeacon!—and has been repeated by historian after historian down through the ages. It was in the school history books when I was a child. For all I know, it may still be in the school history books: we are a conservative people.

Here is David Hume, whose *History of Great Britain*, published between 1754 and 1761, was the first great English history and was for long regarded as a standard work:

> There was one pleasure to which William, as well as all the Normans and ancient Saxons, was extremely addicted and that was hunting; but this pleasure he indulged more at the expense of his unhappy subjects, whose interests he entirely disregarded, than to the loss or diminution of his own revenue. Not content with those large forests, which former kings possessed, in all parts of England, he resolved to make a new forest, near Winchester, the usual place of his residence; and, for that purpose, he laid waste the county of Hampshire, for an extent of thirty miles, expelled the inhabitants from their houses, seized their property, even demolished churches and convents, and made the sufferers no compensation for the injury.

And here is Dr John Lingard, whose *History of England*, published between 1819 and 1830 and written from the viewpoint of enlightened Roman Catholicism, is still regarded as one of the principal authorities from that point of view:

> Though the King possessed sixty-eight forests, besides parks and chases, in different parts of England, he was not yet satisfied, but for the occasional accommodation of his court, afforested an extensive

tract of country lying between the city of Winchester and the sea-coast. The inhabitants were expelled; the cottages and churches were burnt; and more than thirty square miles of a rich and populous district were withdrawn from cultivation, and converted into a wilderness, to afford sufficient range for the deer, and ample space for the Royal diversion. The memory of this act of despotism has been perpetuated in the name New Forest, which it retains at the present day, after a lapse of seven hundred and sixty years.

Writing at about the same time, *circa* 1820, Cooke in his *Geography of Hampshire*, says that "to make his New Forest the Conqueror destroyed many populous towns and villages, and thirty-six parish churches". Shades of Walter Mapes!

William Cobbett, a man of remarkable commonsense—and, it must be admitted, no less remarkable prejudices—had some fun with these historians and their figures. I quote from his *Rural Rides*:

. . . I was about to show that all the historians have told us lies the most abominable about this affair of the New Forest . . . for the historians tell us that, in order to make this Forest, William the Conqueror destroyed "many populous towns and villages, and thirty-six parish churches." The devil he did! How populous, then, must England have been at that time, which was about the year 1090, that is to say 736 years ago! . . . Now, what Hume meant by the loose phrase, "an extent of thirty miles", I cannot say; but this I know, that Dr Lingard's "thirty square miles" is a piece of ground only five and a half miles each way. So that the Doctor has got a curious "district", and a not less curious "wilderness"; and, what number of churches could William find to burn, in a space five and a half miles each way? If the Doctor meant thirty miles square, instead of square miles, the falsehood is so monstrous as to destroy his credit for ever; for, here we have nine hundred square miles, containing five hundred and seventy-six thousand acres of land; that is to say, fifty-six thousand nine hundred and sixty acres more than are contained in the whole county of Berks. This is "history", is it? And these are "historians"?

The true statement is this: the New Forest, according to its ancient state, was bounded thus: by the line going from the river Exe to the river Avon, and which line separates Wiltshire from Hampshire; by the river Avon; by the sea from Christchurch to Calshot Castle,

The idyllic setting of Beaulieu

by Southampton Water; and by the river Exe. These are the boundaries; and (as anyone may, by scale and compass, ascertain) there are within these boundaries about 244 square miles, containing 143,360 acres of land. Within these limits there are now remaining eleven parish churches, all of which were in existence before the time of William the Conqueror; so that if he destroyed 36 parish churches, what a populous country this must have been! There must have been 47 parish churches; so there was, over this whole district, one parish church to every 4¾ square miles. Thus, then, the churches must have stood, on an average, at within one mile and about 200 yards of each other. And observe, the parishes could, on an average, contain no more each than 2,966 acres of land. Not a very large farm! So that here was a parish church to every large farm, unless these historians are all fools and liars.

Good, vigorous, slashing stuff. Not quite accurate, mind you: less accurate, indeed, than Cobbett usually is. There were not, in his day, eleven pre-Conquest churches standing within the ancient boundaries of the New Forest. In fact, there were none. Moreover, to be absolutely accurate, there were not eleven churches within the area when the Conqueror landed on Pevensey Beach: there were none. (The only pre-Conquest church in the area, that at Breamore, was just, if only just, outside the ancient boundary of the New Forest: and that church, as we have seen, stands to this day.) Cobbett may have mis-dated his churches—easy enough to do if you are not expert in architectural matters—but I think that what he actually did was to suppose that a place with a pre-Conquest name must have had a pre-Conquest church. The inaccuracy does not, however, invalidate the argument. Certainly, Cobbett did not intend to mislead.

That, I fear, cannot be said of Dr John Lingard. For he was (as Cobbett was not) a man of learning, a scholar. He was educated at the English Roman Catholic College at Douai and he was, from 1795 to 1811, vice-president of Crookhall College near Durham. In 1806 he published *The Antiquities of the Anglo-Saxon Church*, which suggests that he must have known, approximately at least, the number of Saxon churches standing at the time of the Conquest. Even if he did not, he must have known perfectly well what

6

The open Forest

thirty square miles meant in terms of space. He must have known that there could not have been a word of truth in the story of demolished churches and villages. Moreover, he was born and brought up in the city of Winchester. He must have known the New Forest at least fairly well: well enough to know that it could never, at any time, have been a "rich and populous district".

In so small and thickly populated a country as ours every piece of ground that can be cultivated without too great difficulty is cultivated. Even the Fens, once almost impenetrable, have yielded to man. Only the high mountains, only the bleak moorlands, only the heathlands have defied Man the Cultivator. One would expect that of the mountains and the moorlands; but surely not of the heathlands? For these are confined, for the most part, to south and south-eastern England—to Berkshire, Dorset, Hampshire, Surrey, Sussex—to that part of England which has always, since the earliest times, been comparatively thickly populated. Yet, so it is. Their shallow, sandy, acid soils have always repelled the cultivator. The operative word is "always". There is nothing new in this.

The Saxon farmer—and it must be remembered that, at the time of the Conquest, the population of Britain was only about one million—sought out the loamy, easy soils. There was no pressure on space: he could afford to pick and choose. So he avoided the light, sandy, hungry soils and avoided, too, the heaviest of the clay soils: for example, the Weald, much of which remained covered by dense, wet, oakwoods until late in medieval times. And these areas, since they could not be cultivated, were very sparsely populated: no more than a family or two, a hamlet, in small clearings here and there. This was the type of land—the light, hungry, sparsely populated land—which, in the south and south-west, was used for the Royal hunting grounds. The heavy clay lands were never so used (no part of the Weald, for example, was ever a Royal forest) because, for the greater part of the year, they were much too wet, so deep in mud as to be virtually impassable to horsemen. And closely populated, well cultivated land was never incorporated into a Royal forest. There was never, for example, a Royal forest in the whole county of Kent: sufficient indication that at the time of the Conquest, and for long before, the land there was fully settled and well farmed.

William the Conqueror did not, in fact, "make" the New Forest. It was there already: an area of wretchedly thin soils on which flourished furze and rush, heather and bramble and trees. Part of it, indeed, was a Royal forest in the reign of King Cnut, whose *Canon of Forest Law* was delivered at Winchester in 1016. William the Conqueror did not drive out the inhabitants and he demolished nothing—no trace of a single one of the churches he is supposed to have destroyed has ever been found—all that he did was to enlarge the area subject to Forest law.

"The forest", says Richard fitz Nigel in the *Dialogus*, "has its own laws, based not on the common law of the realm, but on arbitrary legislation by the king." And he goes on to explain why this is so: "In the forests are the secret places of the kings and their great delight. In them they go for hunting, having put off their cares, so that they may enjoy a little quiet. There, away from the continuous business and incessant turmoil of the court, they can for a little time breathe in the grace of natural liberty, wherefore it is that those who commit offences there lie under the royal displeasure along."

William the Conqueror did not interfere with the daily lives of those living in the few small communities scattered through his New Forest. He ordered the afforestation in 1079, twelve years after the Conquest. Seven years later, seven years after the "laying waste" of folk-lore, the great survey for *Domesday* was made. That, and it is the most complete and authentic record that we have, tells us that Saxon thanes still had a number of holdings in the Forest and that corn was being ground at the mills at Bashley, Burgate, and Milford. William did not mind the land in the clearings being tilled and he did not mind pigs being loosed in the woods at acorn-time. He did not interfere, so long as his Forest law was observed. But he that killed a deer died. He that shot at a deer—and missed—had his hands cut off. He that disturbed the deer had his eyes taken from him. Such were William's laws: and for them was William hated.

Huge areas of England were, at this time, subject to Forest Law.

Lady Stenton, in her *English Society in the Early Middle Ages*, points out that "from the Thames, which for many miles was the northern boundary of Windsor forest, a man could in these days pass southwards, bearing in a somewhat westerly direction, through the woods of Eversley or Bagshot into Pamber and so into Bere Forest and finally into the king's New Forest which was bounded by Southampton Water and the Channel coast. Throughout his journey he would be within country which lay under forest law, and far on his either hand forest jurisdiction spread". Almost the whole of the county of Essex was a Royal forest. A great stretch of country, reaching from Oxford to Stamford, was subject to forest law. Delamere Forest included much of the county of Cheshire and the whole of the Wirral Peninsula. There were great forests in Cumberland and Northumberland, in Lancashire and Yorkshire, in Shropshire and Warwickshire and Worcestershire, in Derbyshire and Nottinghamshire, in Gloucestershire and Devon and Somerset. So they stretched, these great areas of land subject to the King's forest law, the length and breadth of England. Evidence enough, some would say, of the King's unbridled passion for hunting.

Not all these forests were on poor ground: far from it. In areas where the population was small and thinly scattered great stretches of good, fertile, thickly wooded country—England was then a very well-wooded land—lay within the boundaries of Royal forests. John Manwood, writing in the sixteenth century (but translating an early Norman work), described these forests as:

stored with great woods or coverts for the secret abode of wild beastes and also with fruitful pastures for their continual feed: for the want of either of these two, doth cause the exile of wild beastes from the Forest to some other place, for that the nature of the wild beaste of the Forest is, to flie into the thicke coverts for places of Secresie to rest in, whereof if there be none within the Forest, then they leave the Forest, and wander up and downe untill they find coverts elsewhere, which being without the bounds of the Forest, where these wild beastes are so found wandering, then they are hunted and killed to the utter destruction of the Forest: and in like

manner it is, if the wild beastes have not those fruitful pastures within the Forest for their feed, then they pine away and starve, or else
they are forced to forsake the Forest and to seek for food without the
Forest, where they can find the same, and then they are likewise
hunted and killed, whence it is manifest that a Forest cannot have
continuance without wooddy grounds and fruitful pastures. And so
consequently it followeth, that to destroy the coverts of the Forest,
is to destroy the Forest itselfe; Also to convert the pasture grounds,
meadowes, and feedings into arable land, is likewise to destroy the
Forest.

A very clear exposition from the huntsman's point of view.

But there was another side to all this: one which is too often
forgotten. It is true that these forests were the playgrounds of the
King, his refuge from the affairs of state. It is true that they were
subject to most ferocious laws, designed to protect animals for the
King's sport. But William the Conqueror was not merely a man
with a passion for hunting (a passion shared by his immediate
successors and particularly by Henry II), was not merely a ruthless
professional soldier who had brought to a successful conclusion
one of the most astonishing adventures in history: he was also a
statesman and a great administrator, who was determined to make
a permanent success of the land he had conquered. His Royal
forests were not set aside solely for his personal enjoyment. They
were part of a deliberate and far-sighted policy. By making these
great tracts of land subject to his Forest laws he was able not only
to control development within them—in his day there was,
indeed, little or no development within them; though it should
not be forgotten that, during his reign, three churches (those at
Boldre, Brockenhurst, and Milford) were built within the
boundaries of the New Forest—but was able to direct development outside them.

William did not interfere with what he found. Within the huge
Forest of Essex there were, as the place names show, many ancient
hamlets and villages. There is no evidence that any one of them
was destroyed: indeed, this was never suggested even by the most
virulent propagandist among the monkish chroniclers. But, under
Forest Law, the amount of land under cultivation around these

hamlets and villages could not be increased. Development had to take place outside the Forest boundaries. Great areas of wild country lay outside the Forest boundaries and were not subject to Forest law—in these areas a man might hunt and slay deer without fear of penalty—and it was in these areas that any additional cultivation had to be undertaken. In the comparatively thickly populated south, for example, there was after the Conqueror's afforestation, so little land available for cultivation, the good land having already been taken up by the Saxons, that men were forced to make inroads into the Weald. William's laws protected the deer, it is true: but it is also true that, but for those laws, the Weald would have remained virtually impassable for much longer than it did. And the same is true of many other parts of England. It could not last, of course—pressure of population would see to that—but this was the policy of the early Normans: of the Conqueror and his universally hated son, William the Red.

Henry I, not surprisingly, avoided the New Forest throughout his reign. But it was he who first granted right of warren to certain subjects whose estates lay within Forest boundaries. Under grant of warren the animals allowed to be hunted and killed were the fox, the wolf, the cat, the hare (rabbits appear to have been included with hares), the badger and the squirrel. It has often been said that these rights were granted for the express purpose of affording additional protection to those animals—the red deer, the fallow deer, the roe deer, and the wild boar—already protected by the Forest law. This shows a lamentable ignorance of natural history. Of the animals that might be hunted and killed under grant of warren, only the fox, the wolf, and the cat—in those days that would, of course, have been the genuine wild cat, which is now confined to the Highlands of Scotland, not the domestic pussy—could have been of any danger to the deer. But the others— the hare and the rabbit, the badger and the squirrel—were of some danger to cultivation, to growing crops (though it is now recognized that the badger is not, that would not have been the case then) and, since the area under cultivation within Forest boundaries was severely restricted and could not be increased, these animals in any numbers were all the greater menace. There can be no doubt that grant of warren, while going some way towards satisfying the pronounced hunting instincts of the people, was not primarily intended to afford additional protection to the deer, but to afford some small measure of protection to the cultivator and so to stifle the rising tide of complaint.

It was not enough. It was not merely that the deer, a constant source of temptation to the poor at a time when meat was scarce, were protected. It was not merely that the deer, which were the greatest single source of damage to the farming interests within the Forest boundaries, damage which affected not only the villagers but their lords also, were protected. It was the fact that the Forest law supplemented the ordinary law of the realm: that those who lived outside the Forest boundary were immune from the penalties oppressing those that lived within it. This was a savage and violent age, an age in which life was regarded cheaply. That a man should be put to death for taking the king's deer probably did not strike anyone as particularly unjust. It was the fact that those living outside Forest boundaries could take deer freely and without fear of the king's foresters that caused deep resentment. Of course, there was a way round the law: there almost always is. It became the custom, wherever possible, to drive deer over the Forest boundary, so that they might be killed without fear of punishment. Naturally, those caught doing this paid the penalty: of blinding or maiming. These two penalties, which were much more bitterly resented than that of death, aroused widespread sympathy for the deer poacher. On more than one occasion a Norman baron—though probably not so much out of sympathy for the man as because a blinded or maimed man was of little use as a workman—intervened with the king's foresters to save a serf from mutilation. Be that as it may, sufficient pressure was exercised in high circles to make Richard I, a king who had not the interests of his English possessions over much at heart, abolish the penalties of blinding and maiming. By so doing he drove the first nail into the coffin of deer protection. Some twenty-five years later Henry III, in his Charta de Foresta, laid it down that in future no man should lose life or limb for a

poaching offence. But by then the whole concept of the Royal
Forest had altered.

For years past pressure on land had been steadily building up.
Henry II, whose passion for hunting was greater even than that
of William the Conqueror, had greatly extended the boundaries
of the Royal Forests and thereby increased, perhaps deliberately
(for he was a great and far-sighted king) the pressure on the
cultivable land. That process obviously could not continue; and
Richard I, who spent almost the whole of his reign abroad and
had, therefore, not the same interest as his predecessors had had in
maintaining the Royal Forests for his pleasure, began the process
of disafforestation. His foreign adventures cost a great deal of
money; and this was one way of raising it. In 1190, the first year
of his reign, the knights of Surrey offered him 200 marks—a huge
sum in those days—"that they might be quit of all things that
belong to the forest from the water of Wey to Kent and from
the street of Guildford southwards as far as Surrey stretches". The
offer was accepted. A large area of Surrey was thus freed from
Forest law, the deer were removed from protection, and the land
could be brought into cultivation. Large scale disafforestation on
similar lines also occurred in one or two areas of the Midlands.
Furthermore, in return for cash, the king turned a blind eye to
"assarts" within the Forest. Richard fitz Nigel defines "assarts" as
"cutting down the forest, woods, and thickets suitable for feeding
animals, ploughing the soil and cultivating it" and he makes it
clear that even the felling of six trees amounted to "assarts". Until
Richard I's day such practices—and one imagines that they were
constantly being attempted on a small scale—constituted an
offence which brought down upon the offender's head some
extreme form of the king's displeasure. Richard I demanded money
for "assarts"—it might be as little as half a mark (nevertheless, a
considerable sum in those days), it was often much more: the
Bishop of Worcester would have had to pay heavily to be
allowed, as he was, to plough up 614 acres of Forest land—and he
always got it. The English were then a land-hungry people, and
somehow the money was always raised. But, naturally, there were
many who took advantage of the relaxation in the Forest laws.

Many unofficial "assarts" must have been made in the huge area
of Royal Forest up and down the country. Towards the end of his
reign, Richard I, short of money as usual, caused a searching
survey to be made of these unofficial "assarts" and many were
caught in the net and made to pay half a mark each. In every case
the fine was paid in full. The important thing, from the point of
view of Forest history, is not that the fines were paid, but that the
offenders, having paid, were left in peace to enjoy the land they
had taken in return for a rent. It meant that the king accepted that
encroachment upon his Forests was inevitable.

The process of disafforestation was continued by King John,
somewhat surprisingly perhaps, since he was extremely fond of
hunting. But he was still more fond of money—during his reign
he acquired a vast treasure—and the cost of disafforestation rose
steeply. In 1204 the men of Essex paid 500 marks and five palfreys
for the disafforestation of "the forest of Essex which is beyond the
causeway between Colchester and Bishop's Stortford". In the
same year the men of Cornwall paid 2200 marks for the disafforestation of the whole county of Cornwall and, a little later, the men
of Devon no less than 5000 marks (an enormous sum) for the
disafforestation of the whole county of Devon. But, at the same
time as this disafforestation was going on, King John seems to
have enlarged the boundaries of the New Forest considerably,
carrying them over the River Avon and, perhaps, as far westward
as to include Poole Harbour. There is, it must be admitted, no
direct evidence for this. But in Henry III's Charta de Foresta it is
specifically laid down that all the land afforested by King John
is to be disafforested at once. Since there is absolutely no evidence
that John afforested land anywhere else within his domains, since
he visited the New Forest a good deal (more frequently than any
king since William Rufus) and since he was often in residence at
his castle at Corfe, this would seem to be the most obvious solution
to the puzzle. Moreover, this was land that no one would be prepared to pay highly to have disafforested.

For King John the Royal Forests were a source both of pleasure
and profit. Though always ready to raise money by allowing disafforestation—at what were, surely, extortionate prices—he was

elsewhere at pains to enforce the Forest law with the utmost rigour, at least so far as the protection of his deer was concerned. For King John the important thing about the Forest was the sport, the venison.

With King Henry III the picture changed. His Charta de Foresta was forced upon him—he was but a child when he came to the throne—by the barons, fresh from their victory of Magna Charta two years before. The barons, no less than the common people, resented the Forest law. They not only took care to disafforest at once all the land, wherever it may have been, afforested by King John, they also undertook in the Charter that all the afforestations made by Henry II should be reviewed by "honest and lawful men" and that only those which were the king's own demesne should be retained as Royal Forests, subject to Forest law. The honest and lawful men did their work thoroughly—they, too, stood to gain by disafforestation and were not overmuch concerned about the king's rights—with the result that during the years immediately following the Charter huge stretches of country were freed from Forest law. In the main, naturally, the lands thus disafforested were good, or reasonably good, lands: lands which could be brought into cultivation without too much difficulty. There was really no point in disafforesting land which was thin and hungry. The New Forest was left to the king.

When he came of age in 1227, Henry III caused another survey to be made of the lands which had been disafforested by the honest and lawful men; with the result that some of these lands were again brought under Forest law. This was done, it would seem, only because Henry wished to assert his authority: for he was not particularly interested in sport. This does not mean to say that he did not protect the deer. On the contrary, by re-afforesting land, he extended that protection. Action against those who killed the king's deer in the king's Forest was still taken. Though a man could no longer lose his life for so doing, he could be, and usually was, cast into prison. But such action was taken, not because the king was passionately fond of hunting—he was not—but because he was anxious to protect his prerogative. Henry III's interest lay not in venison, but in the vert; in the greenwood of the Forest.

In his reign a much more serious view began to be taken of offences against the vert. Such offences as the cutting down of saplings, the lopping of boughs, let alone the felling of grown trees, were matters which had to be reported. Minor offences—lopping of boughs, for example—were punished by fines in the local attachment court. Major offences, which would include the felling of a grown tree and the cutting down of worthy saplings, required the appearance of the offender before the Justices of the Forest and almost always resulted in a heavy fine or a term of imprisonment.

Although his interest in the vert was a great step forward, Henry III had, at the same time, put the clock back by bringing again under Forest law lands which had been disafforested by the honest and lawful men. This action proved a constant source of grievance throughout his reign: the records are full of complaints against the Forest law and the behaviour of Forest officials. But the chief complaint was always against the new boundaries set by the king. So constant was this complaint that Edward I, in 1277, ordered a fresh perambulation to be made. So far as the New Forest was concerned this perambulation made no difference— no one was interested in the disafforestation of thin and hungry soil—but in many places elsewhere the Forest boundaries were re-affixed at those set by the honest and lawful men. Even that was not enough. There was a continual and increasing pressure on land: and men had seen what could be done. In 1297 another perambulation was ordered and again the Forest boundaries were reduced, though again the New Forest was left alone. Three years later, in financial difficulties due to the French and Scottish wars, he was forced in the parliament at Lincoln to agree to further disafforestation; and this time the boundaries of the New Forest were considerably reduced. For what reason is not apparent; for little or no attempt was made to bring the land thus freed into cultivation. It simply was not worth the labour.

Edward I made frequent attempts during the remaining years of his reign to reverse the disafforestations forced upon him by the parliament at Lincoln, but without success. Powerful monarch though he was, he could not, as his father had done, assert his authority in this respect. And it is significant that no monarch thereafter tried to do so. There was no further afforestation by decree of the king. But there was a steady process of disafforestation. Little by little over the years, more and more land subject to Forest law was freed: so that, today, some of the once great Royal Forests are forests only in name—Rockingham Forest and the Forest of Arden, for example—and others are mere fragments of once vast areas, as in the case of Epping Forest (all that is left of the once huge Forest of Essex), Sherwood Forest and Delamere Forest in Cheshire. On the other hand the New Forest boundaries as defined by the parliament at Lincoln in 1300 remained unchanged until the twenty-second year of the reign of Charles II, when they were confirmed. Sufficient indication of the poverty of the soil: and not merely of the New Forest as such, but of the whole heathland, stretching from Southampton Water westwards to Dorchester and from the Channel coast north-eastwards to Windsor Forest and the Thames.

It was for this reason, the poverty of the soil, that for some five hundred years after the parliament at Lincoln, from 1300 to the beginning of the nineteenth century, there is very little definite history connected with the New Forest. This is not to say that no attention was paid to it: but certainly it received much less attention than other Royal Forests situated on better soils. Edward I, though fond of hunting, seems to have been more addicted to falconry than to stag-hunting: at any rate, during his reign the vert was given precedence over the venison. The deer, though important, were no longer regarded as of supreme importance. At the same time, the pressure on land was steadily increasing. This not only meant continual encroachment on the boundaries of the various Royal Forests, it also meant that the demand for material for houses was continually growing. This demand was of two kinds: firstly, for the cottages of the peasants (which were little more than hovels of wattle and daub) for which underwood was required and, secondly, for the more elaborate structures which were beginning to be erected and for which timber was required on a considerable scale. This, to begin with, probably did not happen to any great extent in the New Forest or anywhere else in the great southern heathland, simply because the soil was too poor to make any large-scale settlement worth while, but it did happen to a considerable extent elsewhere and, particularly, in the Midlands. And it led to a very important discovery: that, once cut, the deer and the grazing animals of the local populace never allowed the underwood or seedling trees to grow again. And so the first law affecting silviculture in English history was enacted in 1483. This Act made enclosure legal for a period of seven years. Where the underwood and timber had been cut out on an area, it allowed for a ditch to be dug and a bank thrown up around the area and planted with thorns, so that that area might be protected from the assault of grazing animals until the coppice and seedlings were re-established. It was still, of course, illegal to cut the underwood or to fell timber in a Royal Forest without permission and payment, but it is evident from this Act that the position, since the deer were no longer of supreme importance, had got completely out of hand, that that law could no longer be rigorously enforced. The Act of 1483 accepted the position and tried to make the best of it.

Give a countryman an inch and he will take an ell. Naturally, men took great advantage of this Act. Queen Elizabeth I caused a census to be taken of these enclosures—they were then known as "encoppicements"—and it was found that 5,800 acres in the New Forest alone had been encoppiced: and this total would not, of course, have taken into account those areas which had been thrown open at the end of seven years, areas which had been lost sight of altogether or were indicated only by a few thorns and a crumbling bank. But this considerable acreage does not indicate that there had been much encroachment for settlement in the New Forest (as had been the case in the Forest of Arden and elsewhere in the Midlands), but rather that timber had been taken out for building purposes on the fringes of the heathland or carried for such purposes much further afield. Queen Elizabeth, faced with the Spanish threat, was anxious to conserve a supply of timber for the building of ships and for this purpose the New Forest, close to a number of sea-ports, was ideal. She passed a law—it was called "an act that timber shall not be felled for burning of iron"— which prohibited the felling of trees for charcoal in the New

Forest. (Actually "sea-coal" had already at that time superseded "bavins" and "fire-coal", which is charcoal, for domestic use, but charcoal was still used to a very great extent for the smelting of iron.) And she also instituted a system of enclosures to protect growing timber. Elizabeth, in fact, albeit under pressure of events, showed more interest in the New Forest than had any monarch since King John.

Under the Stuarts the New Forest fell on evil times. James I began by carrying on Elizabeth's policy and, indeed, carried it further. For at his order acorns were gathered and areas of land ploughed up for their planting. But, like so many monarchs before him, James I was soon short of cash. He began giving away the "morefalls" (that is, the windfalls) to various people to whom he owed money: and he even went so far as to pay his officers in trees instead of money. Charles I was always in debt. He continued the policy of giving away the "morefalls" and he even pledged areas of the New Forest as security to some of his creditors. Cromwell did not bother about the New Forest at all: the decay that had set in was allowed to continue. Charles II, inheriting a Forest in decay, was quite unable to do anything about it. A great king in many ways, the last great royal ruler of England, he had inherited not only all the virtues (and they were many) of the Stuarts, but also all their vices. And he was certainly the most spendthrift of them all. He granted the young woods near Brockenhurst to various maids of honour at his court: presumably in return for services rendered. One lady, Frances Wells by name, petitioned the King "to bestow upon her and her children for twenty-one years the morefall trees in three walks of the New Forest" and she also wanted seven or eight acres of ground and ten or twelve trees "wherewith to build her a house". Charles referred this petition to the Lord Treasurer, who strongly disapproved of it and wrote upon the margin: "I conceive this an unfit way to gratify this petitioner." But a year later we find one Winifred Welles, almost certainly a sister of Frances (though it has been suggested that this was Frances herself using a second Christian name, I think that unlikely: Frances was, no doubt, "gratified" in some other way), granted for her own use the King's Coppice at Fawley and New

Coppice and Iron's Hill Coppice at Brockenhurst. On this occasion the King ignored the Lord Treasurer and issued a Royal Warrant on his own account. Evidently the Wells family produced highly attractive, and complacent, daughters who contributed materially to the gaiety of the Court.

Against this, in fairness, it must be stated that Charles II, influenced, no doubt, by Evelyn's *Sylva* and temporarily in funds, did enclose three hundred acres as a nursery for young oaks. But Charles was never in funds for long, and his prodigality and that of his predecessors had its inevitable effect. James II, inheriting little but debts, could barely keep his head above water. For much of his reign the keepers of the New Forest were not paid their wages. As was only natural, they did not bother to care for the trees, which were attacked by rot and, having no shelter-belts to protect them from the great winds off the Channel, suffered greatly. Moreover, they re-imbursed themselves by felling and selling timber. When William III came to the throne the New Forest was in ruins.

William III was a careful and thrifty monarch. He had a great deal to set in order, much leeway to make good and, among all the rest, a fleet that was wearing out. He needed timber and he needed it badly. So the Act of 1698 was passed. This provided for the immediate planting of 2,000 acres in the New Forest and for a further 200 acres per annum, with a final figure of 6,000 acres in mind. This Act gave statutory recognition of Common Rights in the New Forest for the first time and it also provided the King with what later came to be known as the "rolling power" of afforestation: that is, provided that when 6,000 acres had been planted and the trees had grown to a size at which they would be safe from attack from grazing animals, then these acres could be thrown open and a further like acreage enclosed and planted. It was a wise and far-sighted move. But before the work was properly under way there came, in 1703, a great gale. Four thousand of the "best oaks" are said (by Woodward) to have been blown down in this storm. This sounds an exaggeration—the "best oaks" would, one would think, be just the trees to withstand such a storm—but it may well be that the "best" were only the best of a bad lot. At any rate, there can be no doubt that enormous damage was done. You would not think so, reading Defoe who passed through southern Hampshire about 1720. In his *A Tour through England and Wales* he has this to say:

From hence when we came opposite to Southampton, we pass another creek, being the mouth of the river Itchen which comes down from Winchester, and is both very broad and deep, and the ferry men having a very sorry boat, we found it dangerous enough passing it: On the other bank stands the ancient town of Southampton, and on the other side of Southampton comes down another large river, entring Southampton Water by Red-bridge; so that the town of Southampton stands upon a point running out into the sea, between two very fine rivers, both navigable, up some length into the country, and particularly useful for the bringing down timber out of one of the best wooded counties in Britain; for the river on the west side of the town in particular comes by the edge of the great forest, call'd New Forest; here we saw a prodigious quantity of timber, of an uncommon size, vastly large, lying on the shoar of the river, for above two miles in length, which they told us was brought thither from the forest, and left there to be fetch'd by the builders at Portsmouth Dock, as they had occasion for it.

In riding over the south part of Hampshire, I made this observation about that growth of timber, which I mention in supplement to what I said before concerning our timber being wasted and decay'd in England (viz.) that notwithstanding the very great consumption of timber in King William's reign, by building or rebuilding almost the whole navy; and notwithstanding so many of the king's ships were built hereabouts, besides abundance of large merchant ships, which were about that time built at Southampton, at Red-bridge and at Burleston etc. yet I saw the gentlemens estates, within six, eight, or ten miles of Southampton, so over-grown with wood, and their woods so full of large full grown timber, that it seem'd as if they wanted sale for it, and that it was of little worth to them. In one estate at Hursely in particular near Winchester, the estate since bought by Mr Cardonell, late manager for the Duke of Marlborough, and formerly belonging to Mr Cromwell, grandson to Oliver Cromwell, the whole estate not above £800 per ann. in rent, they might have cut twenty thousand pounds worth of timber down, and yet have left the woods in a thriving condition; in an-

Ruins of Beaulieu Abbey

other estate between that and Petersfield, of about £1000 per ann. they told me they could fell a thousand pounds a year in good large timber fit for building, for twenty years together, and do the woods no harm: Colonel Norton also, a known gentleman, whose seat at Southwick is within six miles of Portsmouth, and within three miles of the water carriage; this gentleman they told me had an immense quantity of timber, some growing within sight of the very docks in Portsmouth: Farther west is the like, and as I rode through New Forest, I could see the antient oaks of many hundred years standing, perishing with their wither'd tops advanc'd up in the air, and grown white with age, and that could never yet get the favour to be cut down, and made serviceable to their country.

These in my opinion are no signs of the decay of our woods, or of the danger of our wanting timber in England; on the contrary, I take leave to mention it again, that if we were employ'd in England, by the rest of the world, to build a thousand sail of three deck ships, from 80 to 100 guns, it might be done to our infinite advantage, and without putting us in any danger of exhausting the nation of timber.

Daniel Defoe was normally a shrewd and accurate observer, but one is forced to the conclusion that he did not know a great deal about timber. That, at least, was not the Government's view of the situation—certainly not so far as the New Forest was concerned—and we may be quite sure that, in view of the condition of the Navy, they had surveyed the woodlands in private ownership within easy reach of Southampton and Portsmouth. (Even if the Government's officials had neglected their duty, we may be quite sure that the owners of these heavily wooded estates would have drawn their attention to it: the English country gentleman has never ignored the opportunity of turning an honest penny.) There is, of course, timber and timber: not all large full grown timber was suitable for shipbuilding. In 1707, roughly thirteen years before Defoe's tour, Navy officials made a survey of the New Forest and returned the number of trees fit for shipbuilding at 12,476: a century earlier the figure had been 123,927. Even allowing for the probability that the standard required for shipbuilding had advanced greatly in those hundred years, this is still evidence of a remarkable decline in the fecundity of the New Forest. Yet, so

7

Sign of The Master Builder's at Buckler's Hard

great was the Navy's need, we find in this same year (1707) an order being given that three hundred trees should be felled annually in the New Forest for shipbuilding.

The Act of 1698 plotted the course that should be taken. But very slow progress was made. In the first fifteen years after the passing of the Act only 1,022 acres were planted. A further 250 acres were not planted until 1750. This slow progress was undoubtedly due, in no small measure, to the fact that the "rolling powers" provision aroused violent opposition. Afforestation by the Crown had not been popular in the thirteenth century: it was no more popular in the nineteenth. The English countryman is a very conservative soul.

Despite some planting, and the inroads made by some people who had to be "gratified" by Royalty, the character of the New Forest had altered but little since Norman times. Defoe gives us no picture of the New Forest as a whole, but he does give us this of another part of the great heathland:

From Farnham, that I might take in the whole county of Surrey, I took the coach-road, over Bagshot Heath, and that great forest, as 'tis call'd of Windsor: Those that despise Scotland, and the north part of England, for being full of vast and barren land, may take a view of this part of Surrey, and look upon it as a foil to the beauty of the rest of England; or a mark of the just resentment shew'd by Heaven upon the Englishmen's pride; I mean the pride they shew in boasting of their country, its fruitfulness, pleasantness, richness, the fertility of the soil etc, whereas here is a vast tract of land, some of it within seventeen or eighteen miles of the capital city; which is not only poor, but even quite steril, given up to barrenness, horrid and frightful to look on, not only good for little, but good for nothing; much of it a sandy desert, and one may frequently be put in mind here of *Arabia Deserta*, where the winds raise the sands, so as to overwhelm whole caravans of travellers, cattle and people together; for in passing this heath in a windy day, I was so far in danger of smothering with the clouds of sand, which were raised by the storm, that I could neither keep it out of my mouth, nose or eyes; and when the wind was over, the sand appear'd spread over the adjacent fields of the forest some miles distant, so that it ruins the very soil. This sand indeed is check'd by the heath, or heather, which grows in it, and which is the very common product of barren land, even in the very Highlands of Scotland; but the ground is otherwise so poor and barren, that the product of it feeds no creatures, but some very small sheep, who feed chiefly on the said heather, and but very few of these, nor are there any villages worth mentioning, and but few houses, or people for many miles far and wide; this desert lyes extended so much, that some say, there is not less than a thousand acres of this barren land that lyes all together, reaching out every way in the three counties of Surrey, Hampshire and Berkshire; besides a great quantity of land between Godalming and Petersfield, on the road to Portsmouth, including some hills, call'd the Hind Head and others.

That description would have fitted, perfectly well, the treeless wastes of the New Forest at that time. Indeed, we know that it did: for George III on a journey to Weymouth, half a century later, complained that the moors of the New Forest were more desolate than Bagshot Heath. And Cobbett, writing a century later than Defoe, had this to say:

We had come seven miles across the forest in another direction this morning; so that a poorer spot than the New Forest there is not in all England, nor, I believe, in the whole world. It is more barren and miserable than Bagshot Heath.

And we know that it was very thinly populated, for Defoe himself had recommended to Lord Godolphin that eight hundred poor refugee families from the Palatinate should be settled in the New Forest, there being ample room for them. He worked out a detailed plan for each family to be given a small holding, so that each family might be self-supporting: which is proof enough that he knew as little about soil as he did about timber. That plan, naturally, disappeared into the files. There was space enough in the New Forest, but there was not sufficient reasonably good soil to support a further population, indeed there was none: and the authorities knew it. And this, of course, was the reason for the violent opposition to the "rolling powers" provided for by the 1698 Act. The few "farmers" could see what little reasonably good soil there was disappearing under the "roller": and they did not relish the prospect.

The Government must have reached some accommodation with the Commoners—there is, it must be admitted, no written evidence that they did—because in 1776 a further 2,044 acres were planted. This was the year in which the American colonies declared their independence. It was at this time, too, that we were beginning to build up what was to become the Indian Empire. It was at this time also that Britain was challenging for the command of the seas. Ships—more and more ships (which meant, of course, more and more good oak)—were vital to our continued progress overseas in the face of fierce competition. It has been suggested that the Commoners realized this and were patriotic enough to forego their interest: that they gave up opposition to the "rolling powers". I do not believe that. Men behave like that when they are faced with invasion, with an imminent danger to themselves and their families. They do not behave like that when there is no imminent threat, they are little affected by or interested in affairs on the other side of the world: and this is as true today as it was in the mid-eighteenth century. The opening up of India, for example, would have been of no more than academic interest, if that, to the New Forest Commoner. I am sure that the Government in order to avoid possible (virtually certain) trouble—the destruction of fences, seedlings, and so forth—were at pains to plant in such places as would cause the minimum of hardship to, and therefore the minimum of opposition from, the local populace.

In this year, too, there was one very significant departure from what was then the normal forestry practice. The Scots pine was introduced into the New Forest. The name of the man responsible for this stroke of genius has been lost: and it seems evident that the authorities did not think overmuch of his idea—they were, of course, primarily concerned with the provision of oak for the navy—for the planting was confined to two small plots, one in Bolderwood and the other in Ocknell. But, in fact, this small experiment was destined to change the whole face of the New Forest and, indeed, the whole aspect of the great heathland. For within a very short time the Scots pine was regenerating itself naturally everywhere.

That was 1776: a year of enormous importance in the history of the New Forest and one of great activity within it. But this was only the beginning. The nation's commitments overseas were steadily increasing and were demanding, year by year, a larger and more powerful navy. The timber had to be found somewhere: an inexhaustible supply could not be provided from woodlands already thinned to the point of devastation. Provision had to be made for the future. The Government, therefore, appointed a Royal Commission "to enquire into the state and condition of the woods, forests and land revenues of the Crown". This Commission's first report was issued in 1787 and its fifth, which dealt specifically with the New Forest, in 1789. The Commission recommended reorganization of the government of the New Forest and the continuation of the "rolling powers" provided for in the 1698 Act. There was a good deal of trouble over this—the "rolling powers" provision was passed by the House of Commons, but was rejected by the House of Lords—but finally the 1698 Act was re-enacted in the Act of 1808. A vigorous programme of planting was immediately commenced and by 1848 some 7,000 additional acres had been planted, mostly with oak, though shelter-belts of Scots pine were planted on the exposed sides of the nurseries.

Apart from planting, what was the state of the New Forest at the beginning of the nineteenth century? This is what Mudie had to say about it:

But besides what we have enumerated, there are so many hovels, with minute patches of ground, which have been taken possession of owing to the indifference of the keepers, and are now held by prescription. These encroachers are, generally speaking, persons of very questionable character, who live most wretched and abandoned lives, and procure much of their miserable subsistence by plunder . . . In former times, we believe that this description of population was much more abundant than it is now . . . According to former reports, persons, not in a state of absolutely pecuniary destitution, were in the habit of stealing localities in the forest, which they did by means of hovels, the parts of which were prepared in other places and brought to the forest and erected in the course of a single night.

When once the hovel was erected, and a fire kindled, the keepers could not eject the tenant without the formality of a legal process; and both his ease and his safety were against his having recourse to that. It was a trouble for which he realized no particular advantage; and, as the persons who trespassed upon the forest in this illegal manner were as ready to become murderers as thieves, he was not safe if he interfered with them. This was a wretched state of things, certainly, but that it was the state of things is but too well known. It seems a general law of human nature, that, if a man either remains in the wild forest or returns to it, there is no alternative to his being or becoming a ferocious savage.

A sorry state of affairs indeed! The odd thing is that Cobbett, a most observant man, accustomed to noting the poverty or prosperity of the peasantry wherever he travelled, did not notice it. Throughout his description of the New Forest—and it is a very detailed description—there is no mention of these destitute and ferocious savages. Mudie was all in favour of enclosure, of encroachment upon the forest, provided that it was done by the "upper classes". Cobbett, of peasant stock, was broadly opposed to enclosure of common land. He saw a different picture altogether: not encroachment by the poor by means of hovel (of which there could, in any case, have been very little), but enclosure by the rich. "This forest", he says, "has been crawled upon by favourites, and is now much smaller than it used to be. A time may come, and will come, for inquiring how George Rose, and others, became *owners* of some of the very best parts of this once public property." That time, needless to say, did not come!

Cobbett, travelling the New Forest, shrewdly observant, noted that the deer were the chief cause of trouble, not only to the new plantations, but also to the Commoners. He asks: "For what, and for whom, then, are deer kept in the New Forest; and why an expense of hay-farm, of sheds, of racks, of keepers, of lodges, and other things amounting to more money annually than would have given relief to all the starving manufacturers in the north! And, again I say, who is all this venison and game for?"

Cobbett, not Mudie, gave the truthful picture. It was the rich who were encroaching on the forest and it was the deer that were the chief cause of tension. The deer were steadily increasing in numbers and so were the complaints of the Commoners. So pressing did these complaints become that a Select Committee was appointed to consider them. The result was an Act, known as the Deer Removal Act, which was passed in 1851. This ordered the deer to be destroyed and authorized the Crown, by way of compensation, to enclose a further 10,000 acres for timber production. As soon as the newly planted trees were sufficiently mature, these 10,000 acres were to be thrown open and a further 10,000 acres were then to be enclosed. In other words, the acreage which the Crown was allowed to keep enclosed was increased from 6,000 to 10,000 acres, and the hated "rolling powers" were maintained and on an increased scale.

Not all the deer were destroyed, but the deer removal part of the Act was popular with the Commoners. There was, however, a tremendous outcry about the "rolling powers". The situation was aggravated by the fact that the Deputy Surveyor at the time, Lawrence Henry Cumberbatch, was a young, energetic, dictatorial man, passionately determined to exercise the "rolling powers" to the full without concern for the interests of the residents. (He did, in fact, enclose and afforest 10,000 acres between 1851 and 1868.) The outcry caused by the activities of Mr Cumberbatch was so great that it became known as the Commoners' Revolt. In fact, it was much more than a Commoners' revolt. The Commoners' protest was, as formerly, based mainly on economic grounds. Alone such a protest would have caused little more than a nuisance. But now the Commoners were joined by those of the "gentry" who had achieved private enclosure within the forest and by those who, increasingly, were settling on the confines of the forest in order to enjoy its beauty. The complaint of these newcomers was based chiefly on aesthetic grounds. The iron-clad was replacing the old wooden ship, the demand for oak was not so insistent, more and more conifers were being planted: the character of the New Forest was being changed and the new residents, gentry and middle-class alike, did not relish the change. Commoners and new settlers together presented a formidable front, for many of the new residents were people of wealth and influence with access to the seats of power. No fewer than eight appeals were taken to the House of Lords in 1867 alone. Such pressure could not be withstood. In 1871 the House of Commons decreed that no more old trees were to be felled and no new enclosures made within the boundaries of the New Forest pending an enquiry into the whole problem. In 1875 yet another Select Committee was set up. Of its deliberations was born the New Forest Act of 1877.

This Act made three major changes. Firstly, it clarified the hitherto ill-defined and bitterly disputed power of the Crown. It set forth beyond question the rights of the silvicultural depart-ment to future enclosure. It abolished the "rolling powers", lay-ing down that no more land could be enclosed beyond that enclosed in the reign of William III and subsequently up to the passing of this Act. (This meant, of course, that the area still allowed to be enclosed at any one time was 16,000 acres.) Secondly it protected the Commoners in the exercise of their admitted rights. Thirdly, it reconstituted the ancient Court of Verderers, so that it became representative of the Commoners and was able to protect their privileges. The 1877 Act, in fact, met all the Commoners' complaints and redressed all their grievances.

Mr Cumberbatch retired in 1880. He had come to the New Forest in 1849 and his thirty-one years of office were very troubled for in his enthusiasm for his job he succeeded in getting himself heartily disliked. But it must be said for Mr Cumberbatch that he virtually made the New Forest that we see today. He was a great forester, a little ruthless perhaps, but wise and far-seeing. He planted a great deal of Scots pine—which proved very valuable to the nation in the second World War—and he introduced the green Douglas fir. Many of these were felled during the second World War, but many are still standing, fine mature trees of 130 feet or so. Cumberbatch, indeed, introduced many new trees to the New Forest and it was he who established the collections of specimen trees, which may be seen today in Bolderwood Grounds, four miles west of Lyndhurst, and along the Ornamental Drive, which starts two-and-a-half miles south-west of Lyndhurst on the Bournemouth road. But Cumberbatch also planted a great deal of oak with shelterbelts of Scots pine. Many of the fine oakwoods which we see today are due to him. He does not deserve to be remembered only in connection with the Commoners' Revolt.

Cumberbatch was succeeded by the Hon. Gerald Lascelles, who was to reign for thirty-five years, 1880–1914. Lascelles, too, was a young man when he took over and he had a most uncomfortable time to begin with. The Commoners had just won a bitter battle with the Office of Woods. That Office had not shown itself conciliatory in the past and had ridden roughshod over many accepted privileges. The Commoners were, not unnaturally, suspicious of the new régime and it must be admitted that they took every opportunity of irritating the forest officials. They had plenty of opportunity, too, for the 1877 Act was not a good job of parliamentary draughtsmanship and left many minor points open to interpretation. Lascelles was, of course, the chief sufferer.

But Lascelles was the right man in the right place at the right time. An aristocrat, he had a natural sympathy with the wealthy landlords, but he also understood, from the very nature of his upbringing, the Commoners and treated them always—so long as they kept their place!—with courtesy and respect.

Lascelles' chief worry was over the roads, which he was anxious to see improved. There might have been real trouble here, for the Commoners maintained that the old forest tracks, fords, and crossings were good enough for them as they had been good enough for their forefathers. They had no need for made-up roads, for bridges, for culverts. They were quick to point out that the only heavy traffic in the New Forest was the timber-haulage of the Office of Woods. They did not see why they should pay for the upkeep of roads they did not need. The Office of Woods, said the Commoners bluntly, should pay for their own roads. And if the new roads were needed for the new gentry, who were buying the houses, lodges, and cottages put up for sale by the Office of Woods—well, they did not want the gentry either. They made it very plain that they were not going to pay a penny. But this time the gentry were not at one with the Commoners: they were prepared to pay. Lascelles did not think it fair that the gentry should pay if the Commoners did not, and he knew well enough that the Commoners' purses were shallow. He was not prepared to face another show-down with the Commoners. The New Forest Highways Act, which behind the scenes he did a good deal to further, provided that the Crown should put the old roads into good condition and build the new roads, and that thereafter both should be maintained by the Road Boards. The Commoners were delighted with this arrangement. But, shortly afterwards, the roads became the responsibility of the County Council (a new body at that time), so they had, through the County Council Rates, to contribute to the upkeep of the roads after all. There was no trouble. The Commoners were not paying the Office of Woods: and that made all the difference.

Lascelles ruled the New Forest for thirty-five years. Unlike Cumberbatch, he left little mark, silviculturally, on the forest. He maintained a high standard of fencing and drainage, he built some new bridges and, of course, it was due to him that the road system was put in order. Above all, he maintained peace. He arrived in an atmosphere of suspicion. Unlike Cumberbatch, he retired greatly loved; especially by the Commoners, who had learned that, though he could be firm and very bluntly spoken, he was always just. Some measure of his stature may be gauged from the fact that another New Forest Act was not required until 1949.

And that brings us to modern times.

V

THE NEW FOREST: PERAMBULATION

WE were at Breamore. There are ways into the Forest from here, for example, through Woodgreen, and there are ways into the Forest from Fordingbridge just to the south. But the sensible thing to do is to go further south, to Ringwood, and to take the main road (A31) to Cadnam. On this road you climb uphill to Picket Post and, though this is not in fact at all high in terms of feet above sea level, you get from the ridge here the most extensive views on either hand: southwards to the Isle of Wight on a clear day, north-westwards to Cranborne Chase, northwards to Salisbury Plain. A little further on is Stoney Cross, notable only for a good hotel, then a short stretch of Roman road running as straight as a die, and then a turning to the left (signposted), which leads to the Rufus Stone.

The Rufus Stone is visited by almost everyone who goes to the New Forest and, I should guess, by every American. It has always struck me as a great pity that the Americans, at any rate, should come so far to see so singularly unimpressive an erection, for the stone has been encased in cast-iron to protect it from those tourists with a yen for scratching their initials or ruder messages on lavatory walls and public monuments. The inscription on this sorry monument reads:

Here stood the oak tree on which an arrow shot by Sir Walter Tyrrell at a stag glanced and struck King William the Second surnamed Rufus on the breast of which he died instantly on the second day of August *anno* 1100.

King William the Second surnamed Rufus being slain as before related was laid on a cart belonging to one Purkis, and drawn from hence, to Winchester, and was buried in the Cathedral Church of that city.

That the spot where an event so memorable might not hereinafter be forgotten the enclosed stone was set up by John Lord Delaware who has seen the tree growing in this place.

The stone was not erected until 1745, and it must be said that it is very problematical if it, indeed, marks the actual spot where the King died. But here or hereabouts died unmourned the most savage of all our kings.

The inscription is a brief summary of the account left us by the chroniclers. Here, in greater detail, is the story told by those worthy, but not always accurate (for they were careful, living in dangerous times, to keep their eye on the main chance) gentlemen, who, if they disagree on some minor points of detail, are agreed upon the main outline.

According to the chroniclers, Rufus and a small party—composed of his brother Henry, Sir Walter Tyrrell, Robert FitzHamon, William de Breteuil, and a few others—set out to hunt in the morning. They hunted all morning and afternoon and, as the sun was going down, a stag bounded past. The King shot and slightly wounded it; and as it ran he watched it, shading his eyes with his hand. Another deer broke cover and one of the party—popularly supposed to have been Sir Walter Tyrrell (William of Malmesbury says that at this time the King was alone with Tyrrell, but Vitalis maintains that there were others present)—shot an arrow, which lodged in the King's breast. He tried to pull it out, but it broke off short in his hand, and he fell dead without uttering a sound. Immediately the party fled in all directions. Henry galloped to Winchester to have himself proclaimed king before anyone could put in a word for his brother Robert. William de Breteuil followed him—rather slowly, it must be admitted—and proclaimed the right of Robert, then in the Holy Land, as lawful successor. Sir Walter Tyrrell crossed the Avon near Ringwood, made for the coast, and sailed to Normandy. The others, presumably, went home and kept quiet. Nobody bothered about the dead king. Rufus lay where he fell until a charcoal burner, named

Purkis—a New Forest name to this day—put the body into his cart and brought it into Winchester.

That is the story. When I was a boy I was taught—maybe schoolchildren are still so taught—that the arrow shot by Sir Walter Tyrrell glanced off an oak; that the whole affair was an accident, albeit a fortunate one. But was it?

William the Conqueror bequeathed his throne to his second son, William Rufus, because he realized that his eldest son, Robert Duke of Normandy, was too gentle a character to rule a recently conquered country. Rufus was not a gentle character: he was a most unpleasant person. William of Malmesbury describes his personal appearance: "He was small and thick-set and ill-shaped, yet having enormous strength. His face was redder than his hair, and his eyes were of two different colours. His vices were branded on his face." His strength, indeed, was such that no man but himself could draw his bow. And as for his vices: he was a man of insatiable sexual appetite, a lover of women, young and old, a homosexual and a sadist who delighted (as did King John in later years) in witnessing torture. In his reign the Forest law—and especially in the New Forest, which was his favourite hunting ground—was enforced even more stringently, against peer and peasant alike, than under the Conqueror. He was hated by his barons and he was hated by the Church because he had a habit of refusing to appoint new abbots and bishops when sees fell vacant, appropriating their dues to himself. But there is no evidence that he was particularly hated by the native, the conquered, population. No Norman was liked, of course. Two members of the Royal family—Rufus's brother Richard and his nephew, another Richard—met sudden death in the Forest, and it is extremely improbable, no matter what the chroniclers may say, that either death was accidental. But a strong king, even though a vicious one, though not loved, was approved by the native population because he kept the barons in order and it was the barons who were the immediate oppressors. It is probable that the two Richards fell victim to the arrows of outraged peasants. But killing minor Royalty was one thing, killing a king quite another. If this was murder, it was not murder by the natives.

And it was murder. There can be no doubt about that. It was murder; deliberate, well-planned murder. Everything points to it. The dreams of the monks before the event, as recorded by the chroniclers, are obvious embellishments and may be disregarded. But one cannot disregard the fact that Fulcred preached a sermon about the King being killed by an arrow on the day before the King was, in fact, killed by an arrow. Nor can one disregard the fact that news of the King's death in the New Forest was known in France before he was dead.

It was murder beyond a doubt. But it will never be known who was the murderer. This is one of the great mysteries of history. But, personally, I think that the suspects can be reduced to two.

Sir Walter Tyrrell's hurried departure for France—he certainly lost no time at all—has always been taken as a tacit admission that he shot the fatal arrow, as an admission of guilt. But there is another explanation. He may well have thought (a not unnatural supposition) that Robert, the eldest son of the Conqueror, and therefore the rightful heir, would succeed. Thinking so, he would be eager to be the first to bring the glad tidings to the Norman court, thereby staking a good claim to a place in the royal favour and some position at Robert's court. Tyrrell, it must be remembered, always denied that he shot the arrow. Moreover, he denied doing so on his death-bed in the presence of priests: not, in those superstitious days, the action of a guilty man. He may well have known what was going to happen—his actions suggest that he did —but he must, I think, be acquitted of murder.

And so must William de Breteuil. Indeed, of all those present he seems to have been the only one who did not know what was going to happen. After the killing he obviously took some time to make up his mind what to do, but he then rode into Winchester to proclaim Robert, the rightful heir, as king. To do so, knowing that Henry was ahead of him, probably already there, knowing the temper of the family, required enormous courage. This, surely, was the action of a good man taken by surprise: not that of an assassin.

The arrow may, of course, have been loosed by some person unknown, by a hired assassin. I think this possibility may be discarded straightaway. Too many people knew well in advance that the killing was scheduled for August: the Church certainly did. So important a task as the assassination of a king, and so ruthless a king as William Rufus, would not have been entrusted to a hired killer. That would only have been done had the King been a prisoner—hired assassins were used for both Edward II and Edward V—but not for a king at large and at the height of his power. The risk of discovery, of a premature leakage of the plot, would have been altogether too great.

We are left with FitzHamon and Henry. FitzHamon cannot be acquitted. He disappears from history with quite remarkable abruptness. He was, we know, present at the time of the killing: but we do not hear another word about him. And that is significant. Perhaps it is a little too significant? If he was the murderer, and Henry was not a party to the murder plot, surely he would have acquired righteousness by hunting down and killing his brother's murderer? He did nothing of the sort. On the other hand, if he was party to the plot and FitzHamon the actual murderer, then surely he would have taken steps to dispose of him as quickly as possible: he would have been altogether too dangerous a man to have around. But, even for a Norman king, it would have been virtually impossible to eliminate a powerful baron without somebody knowing about it. There would surely have been a rumour, a whisper. There is nothing, not a word. FitzHamon just disappears. And that leaves us with Henry.

The case against the saintly Henry is black indeed. He acted with quite remarkable promptitude, without any hesitation. One cannot escape the conclusion that he knew what was going to happen and exactly what he must do when it did. He caused no enquiry to be made into his brother's death: he made no attempt to punish anyone. He was content to bury his brother as quickly as possible and no questions asked. He had no qualms about breaking his oath of fealty to his elder brother, Robert. He had no qualms about marrying a nun. He was not, in fact, as saintly as the chroniclers of the time would, for their own safety, have us believe. I do not say that Henry drew the bow (though I think it possible, even probable), but I do say that he knew it was to be drawn at some time that day.

From the Rufus Stone return to the main road—it is dual-carriage way now and you cross a cattle-grid to get on to it—and turn left for Cadnam. At the Cadnam roundabout, crossing another cattle-grid, take the road to Lyndhurst.

Lyndhurst is the 'capital' of the New Forest and makes an admirable centre for exploring the whole. Of course, the only real way to explore the New Forest is on foot. But if you have not the time to do this and wish to get the feel of the Forest in the space of an afternoon, then choose an afternoon in autumn (when the colouring is at its best), take the Bournemouth road as far as Wilverley cross-roads, turn right there and take the Burley road and follow it through to Picket Post, where you again turn right on to the Cadnam road and so back to Lyndhurst. This comparatively short drive includes almost every variety of Forest scenery, and in the whole length of it there is only the one village, Burley.

I have said some harsh things about Lyndhurst in my time: deserved when said. When the motor-car and the motor-coach first brought tourists in large numbers to this little village—and, as it stands at the junction of many roads, the influx at the height of summer was, and is, immense—Lyndhurst became an exceptionally unpleasant place. There was money to be made out of the tourists. Lyndhurst set about making it, and did so as crudely and as rudely as the most brash seaside resort. It was as though the local shopkeepers could not believe that this manna from heaven would continue to fall into their laps; as though they were convinced that they must grab all they could without losing a moment, even the moment taken in passing a polite word. But now the "gold rush fever" has been stilled. The tourists still come in their thousands, pass through in thousands more—at week-ends in summer Lyndhurst can boast traffic jams as bad as any in Hampshire—but now they are taken as a matter of course. Lyndhurst has settled down again: has now time for the polite word.

Lyndhurst is not a beautiful village. It is made up of one long street of shops and pubs with a luxury hotel at either end, a number of solidly-built, detached, comfortable Victorian villas and a larger number of smaller houses in the modern manner, and two buildings which should not be missed: the church and the King's House.

The saltings near Lepe

Not that there is much chance of missing the church, which has a very tall spire and stands on a knoll. It is a most conspicuous object: and I use the word deliberately. This large red brick building was erected in 1863 on the site of a smaller—and, judging by a drawing in Mudie's *Hampshire*, much more suitable—early Georgian church. It is completely out of keeping with its forest surroundings: in this situation, an utterly preposterous building. But it is obviously much loved locally, for the spacious interior is most beautifully kept. Every time I have been in, and I have been many times, I have been struck by its cleanliness.

Why, if I think the building utterly preposterous, do I go time and again? For three reasons: the great wall painting beneath the east window, the glass in the east and south transept windows, and the memorial to Sir Charles Jennings at the west end of the north aisle. This is a panel by Flaxman, the date 1826 (it was removed from the earlier Georgian church), showing a woman bowed in grief over a broken column. I think it is an exquisite thing; in taste and design infinitely superior to the other memorials in this church. The glass is by William Morris to the design of Burne-Jones and is superb of its kind. The wall painting is a gigantic work by Lord Leighton, representing the Parable of the Ten Virgins. It is poorly lighted—strange, when you think of all the money that has been spent on Lyndhurst church—so that the full effect of the rich colouring is lost, and it must be said that the rather garish surroundings—the whole interior may properly be described as "richly" decorated—do not help. But this is a remarkable work and does repay study. The artist, by the way, used local girls as his models. The foolish virgins, in their distress, are pretty and dainty. The models must have been very pleased with the artist. A local woman was also used as model for the restraining angel, who has a stern and most forbidding countenance. I doubt if she was quite as pleased. In the churchyard lies Mrs Reginald Hargreaves, whose maiden name was Alice Liddell. She was the original of *Alice in Wonderland*, the

> Child of the pure unclouded brow
> And dreaming eyes of wonder.

New Forest pony stallions fight for their mares
Red Deer stag, hind and calf near Brockenhurst

The King's House, a fine late Jacobean brick building standing near the church, used to be the official residence of the Lord Warden of the Forest. The main building has been modernized and is now the office of the Forestry Commission. But the hall in which the Verderers' Court is held is of original date and contains some furniture which is certainly very much older. The long dark hall has on its walls the heads of many deer, none of them very old, and also a piece of rusted iron, which is known as Rufus's Stirrup. It is certainly a stirrup iron, but one of unusual size, measuring ten and a half inches by seven and a half inches. This is said to have been used as the measure through which all dogs in the Forest had to pass if they were to escape "lawing". The practice of *expediation*, or lawing, began, so far as is known, in the reign of Henry III and was designed to protect the deer from the depredations of large dogs, which were kept by the local people and undoubtedly used for poaching. If the dog could not pass through the measure—and nothing bigger than a terrier could get through this stirrup iron—then three claws were struck off each of the fore-paws. This rendered the dog harmless to the deer, but did not, of course, prevent it from herding cattle or acting as a watch-dog. Anyway, Rufus's Stirrup was not (as one legend has it) used by William Rufus on the day he was murdered nor was it used as an expediation measure in the reign of Henry III. It is of seventeenth-century date; probably Cromwellian.

Lyndhurst may have been an ecclesiastical parish in the thirteenth century, but from that time until 1928 it was, despite the size of its church, no more than a chapel of the rectors of Minstead. So one ought next to visit Minstead, and this is easily done by taking the Cadnam road and turning left just beyond the Kennels. Minstead church, like Lyndhurst church, is set upon a knoll: unlike Lyndhurst church it is small and white-washed and exactly right, fitting its surroundings perfectly.

Architecturally Minstead church is a positively astonishing jumble of styles. The original building was Norman and there is a very fine Norman font, which has on its west face the Baptism of Christ, on the east face the Agnus Dei, on the north face two lions with a joint head, and on the south face two eagles. This remarkable and finely carved font has also a remarkable story attached to it. It was dug up, in the course of ordinary horticultural activities, in the rectory garden; which must have caused the rector of the time considerable surprise. The north doorway and the chancel arch are Early English, though the chancel arch is built in part of rounded Norman stones. The base of the chancel screen is fifteenth century, the north porch seventeenth century, the brick tower eighteenth century, and the south transept early nineteenth century. A small doorway in the north porch leads to two family pews: those of Castle Malwood and Minstead Lodge. (It was at Castle Malwood that William Rufus is said to have lodged the night before he was murdered.) These two pews are built like small rooms, for they are backed by large windows and one has a fireplace. Once in them the worshippers are completely hidden from the rest of the congregation, but not from the eye of the preacher. Some of the plain, roughly hewn (you can see the adze marks on some of them), oak pews in the body of the church are certainly at least three hundred years old. There is a great three-decker pulpit (a rare feature in English parish churches) a double tier of galleries, so low that a normal-sized man must stoop to pass. Such a hotch-potch, crammed into so small a space as this (the whole thing is really not very much bigger than a cottage), could easily make a horrible eyesore: in fact, the whole blends perfectly. I do not think that anyone could, truthfully, describe Minstead church as beautiful, despite the attractiveness of its setting with the big yew at the gate—one could not, indeed, expect beauty in its pure sense in such an assortment—but I do not think that anyone would deny that it is lovely: lovely as an old and loved woman is lovely. There is about Minstead church nothing cold. It has the homely atmosphere of, is as warmly welcoming as, a farmhouse kitchen. I mean nothing disrespectful. Is not that just what one should feel about an old and much used village church?

In the vault under the chancel lie the Comptons. Comptons, for more than two hundred years, have been squires and rectors of Minstead. One Canon Compton was rector for fifty-six years and no less than five have held the living. Among them lies one who was not a Compton, one who had no connection whatsoever with the family—an Earl of Errol. There is a strange story about this. It is said that the Earl died so heavily in debt that his creditors seized his body to prevent its burial; though what they hoped to gain by doing so I cannot imagine, unless they thought they might sell it to one of the hospitals and that would not have done much to pay off the debt. Anyway, the then Squire Compton, an old man, heard about it. He went over to the Earl's house and sat by the body and prevented it being taken away; and the next day he brought it to the manor and gave it burial in his own vault. A truly Christian action. I hope it is a true story: I think it is.

Minstead churchyard with its fine yews and good headstones is one of the most restful places I know. Sitting in the churchyard you look over the village green—where the ponies graze and men play cricket, where young men meet their sweethearts and old men doze in the sun—is the Trusty Servant Inn. The sign is a copy of the early seventeenth-century picture by John Hoskyns, which hangs in Winchester College. It shows a man with the ears of an ass on a pig's head, the snout of which is padlocked, and the feet of a stag. The right hand is held out and open, the left carries shovel, pitchfork, broom and grid-iron, while a sword hangs from the left hip and a shield can be seen above the right shoulder. The inscription reads.

> A Trusty Servant's portrait would you see,
> This emblematic figure well survey.
> The Porker's snout not nice in diet shows,
> The Padlock shut no secret he'll disclose.
> Patient the Ass his Master's wrath will bear,
> Swiftness in errand the Stag's feet declare;
> Loaded his Left Hand apt to labour saith;
> The Vest his neatness, Open Hand his faith.
> Girt with his Sword, his Shield upon his arm
> Himself and Master he'll protect from harm.

Above the village, northwards, in the direction of the Rufus Stone which lies beyond the Roman road, is the tree-covered knoll of Castle Malwood. There was never a castle here: the name has come from the rudimentary earthwork on the crown of the knoll, which may have been an Iron Age hill-fort, but which was probably a cattle corral. Quite apart from this and the possibility that William Rufus (and, presumably, his killers) may have lodged here the night before his murder, Castle Malwood has played a most significant part in British history. Castle Malwood House was the home of the Harcourt family. It was Sir William Harcourt, Chancellor of the Exchequer in 1894, who introduced death-duties: a step which was to alter the structure of British society and change the face of Britain. Castle Malwood House has now been taken over by the Electricity Board: a fitting retribution.

Let us return to Lyndhurst and take the road to Beaulieu. Immediately, on your left hand, you pass Bolton's Bench—a Round Barrow, now tree-covered and barely recognizable as such—and then drive over moorland, great woodlands away to your right, a matter of three miles or so to Beaulieu Road Station. Beyond the station, just past the left-hand fork to Dibden, there lies, on the right of the road, a patch of marshy ground, perhaps a mile in length and a little less than half-a-mile wide at its broadest point, which is enclosed by a dyke, known as the Bishop's Ditch. The story goes that the King granted "as much land in the New Forest as the Bishop of Winchester, on his hands and knees, could crawl round in a day". He must have thought, having regard to the normal conformation of bishops, that he was not going to lose much land. But this bishop was an athletic man and a keen sportsman. He chose the best bit of snipe-shooting in the Forest, took advantage of a rather foolish slip on the part of His Majesty, who had said "in a day" instead of (as he undoubtedly meant) "in daylight", and crawled round it in twenty-four hours. It is a good story and it conjures up a pleasing picture. But, in fact, the irregular shape of this area of marshy ground—in places it is no more than a couple of hundred yards wide—suggests that the dyke was built to enclose a shallow pond: that this was originally a fish-pond.

Beyond the Bishop's Ditch is Woodfidley. Lyndhurst people have a proverb about Woodfidley rain: if rain clouds are seen coming from the direction of Woodfidley, that is, roughly from the south-eastwards, then it will be Woodfidley rain. In other words, it will rain steadily and drenchingly all day long. Woodfidley must have some special power over the clouds, for the same saying holds good at Brockenhurst, which lies to the south-west of Woodfidley, and at Beaulieu, which lies to the south-east!

Returning to the main road, there is a couple of miles more of moorland and then you run through woods to pick up the Beaulieu River and so, following its course, come to Beaulieu itself at the head of a wide, open reach. Beaulieu has everything: history, a ruin, a river, a beautiful name. It ought to be spoilt. Despite everything, it is not.

The ruins are the ruins of an abbey: the one and only abbey founded by King John, and founded, so it is said, because of a dream. Tradition has it that in 1204 some Cistercian monks at Lincoln had the temerity to appeal in person to the King for relief. King John, not a charitable man by nature, flew into a rage at their impudence—he was subject, all his life, to bursts of uncontrollable rage—and ordered his horsemen to ride them down: and this they did, trampling the monks to death. That very night the King dreamed: and dreamed that he himself was brought to trial, condemned, and flogged. So vivid, so real was the dream, that when he woke his body bore traces of the punishment he had received. Being told that this nocturnal visitation was a sign that God was displeased with him, he decided to expiate his sin by founding a monastery for the Cistercians. The place he chose was Bellus Locus, and the monastery he founded was to become one of the proudest and most powerful of all English abbeys. Maybe, the story of that dream is but another piece of superstitious folk-lore; certainly his subsequent career does not suggest that King John was ever troubled by conscience—and I am, I must admit, inclined to doubt that bit about the marks of the flogging, but I think that he may well have had a nightmare that night and I think that the incident may have remained with him throughout his life, although it was never allowed to interfere either with his political activities or with his personal appetites. I think so because there is some indirect evidence that at the end this undeniably brilliant, but basically evil man was stricken with conscience; was, perhaps, just a little afraid. At any rate, he took the precaution to have himself buried between two saints: a sort of insurance, I fancy, against too painful a life after death.

King John died, of course, long before his monastery was completed. The great church was consecrated in 1227, but the whole took forty-two years to complete (and that was very quick work indeed), so that what may be described as the opening ceremony did not take place until 1246, when it was dedicated by the Bishop of Winchester, who was assisted by the Bishops of Wells, Chichester and Exeter, in the presence of Henry III (the son of the founder) and his Queen, the royal children, and a great train of nobles and prelates. Their entertainment must have cost Hugh, the first abbot, a sum that in terms of today's money would represent a small fortune.

Beaulieu Abbey was built with stone from Quarr in the Isle of Wight and stone from Caen in Normandy. There is a tradition that the Isle of Wight stone was brought in carts at low tide across a causeway which then existed between the island and a point near Lepe. The authorities, I understand, deny the existence of this causeway, dismissing it as legendary. I do not know. But I think that old stories which have been handed down verbally from generation to generation are often at least as reliable as much of the written history of long ago. (We have already seen how much reliance can be placed on some of the statements contained in the old chronicles.) I think that there may well have been a causeway, perhaps usable only at spring tides—if not between Lepe and the island, perhaps between Hurst and the island—but, if there was, I doubt if it was used to bring Quarr stone to Beaulieu. It would have been much more convenient, and a great deal cheaper, to use the tidal river and bring it direct to the site.

It is difficult to realize now how monumental was the task that was undertaken. It is difficult to realize now that, when the Cistercians first came to Beaulieu, there was nothing in the neighbourhood; nothing at all, not even a hamlet. There was nothing but forest, nothing but a wilderness, which stretched unbroken as far north as Windsor. Before anything could be done, the site had to be cleared; an army of men must have been employed to do this properly. If the stone was brought by water, then quays must have been built for its unloading. And then, a great company of men must have been employed on the actual building. This army of men had to be housed and fed. And it must be remembered that, to start with at any rate, all the food had to be brought to the site, for there was no cultivated land. There must have been a vast array of temporary buildings in use while the site was being cleared and while the permanent buildings of the Abbey were being erected. And, among the original band of monks, there must have been an organizing genius.

Work did not cease with the completion of the Abbey buildings, of course. When that was done, the precinct wall, parts of which can still be traced to the north and east of the Abbey ruins, was built; and that in itself was a monumental task. When the wall was finished the whole estate of some ten thousand acres was surrounded by a ditch and a great earth bank, which may be seen pretty well intact, at the present day. Ten thousand acres: just imagine what that means in terms of digging a ditch and throwing up a bank!

But, of course, at the time these tremendous tasks were undertaken, life was a little easier. The Cistercians were not only magnificent builders, they were also expert agriculturalists. We may be sure that, as soon as humanly possible, Beaulieu, naturally well-watered, was self-supporting. Evidence of the skill of these monks as agriculturalists may be seen in the great barn at St Leonards (three and a half miles to the south of the Abbey) in which they stored their wool and their harvests. Originally, this barn measured 210 feet by 70 feet. Mere figures do not really mean very much. What you should do is to go and stand inside what is left and remember that what is left is about one-fourth of the original. I think, remembering that, you will be very impressed. In fact, when this barn stood in its entirety, it would have taken within its walls and beneath its roof a decent-sized parish church, tower and all, and was the largest barn in Britain. No one, not even a Cistercian master-builder with a size complex, would build a barn that size for no reason at all. It is very evident that, under the Cistercians, this was an exceptionally productive estate.

Beaulieu Abbey had a great reputation for hospitality and was much used by travellers of all degrees of rank from Royalty and nobility downwards. Since it lay well off the beaten tracks across a most desolate region many a traveller must have gone well out of his way to make sure of a good meal and lodging. But more important, Beaulieu, under rights granted by Pope Innocent III, was one of the five principal sanctuaries in England. Here came Queen Margaret of Anjou and Anne Neville, Countess of Warwick, after the Battle of Barnet, in which Warwick the Kingmaker was killed. Queen Margaret is said to have nipped over the precinct wall, got on to a boat, and escaped down the river to France. Anne Neville stayed for fifteen years, safe in sanctuary. Perkin Warbeck, the pretender to the throne, who was a thorn in Henry VII's side for fourteen years, also sought sanctuary here after his disastrous campaign in Cornwall in 1497. He, too, could have stayed for his life-time in perfect safety. But, after two years, he was enticed beyond the wall and paid for his trust on the scaffold.

But it was not only the politically important who sought sanctuary here. All manner of men, criminals and debtors, sought safety at Beaulieu and lived in the grounds with their wives and families. And there can be no doubt that they caused the abbots a good deal of trouble. In 1533, when a new abbot was to be elected, it was recommended that he should be "a man of great gravity and circumspect, and not of base stomach or faint heart when need shall require. The place stands so wildly, it is a great sanctuary and boundeth upon a great forest and upon the sea coast where many sanctuary men may do great displeasure if they be not well and substantially looked for". In other words—in simple, modern, English—it was recommended that the new abbot should be "tough".

At the Dissolution the place was sold to Thomas Wriothesley, first Earl of Southampton, an ancestor of the Montagu family who own Beaulieu today. He demolished most of the buildings and sold the stones of which they were built. He left standing only the Great Gate House (which he converted into a dwelling-house and which is now the seat of Lord Montagu of Beaulieu and known as Palace House), the porter's lodge, the cloisters, the dormitory of the lay brothers, and the monks' refectory, which has long been used as the parish church. The stones he sold were used for the building of Hurst Castle and Calshot Castle at either end of the Solent and for building a residence for the Governor of the Isle of Wight, the house which is now the premises of the Royal Yacht Squadron.

Thinking of what once stood there, of the magnificent church that was built, looking at these ruins, one cannot help but feel sad; cannot help but wonder at the apparently senseless violence that was part of the "glorious Reformation". It must be remembered that the Dissolution of the Monasteries was also an exercise in "nationalization", that there was a political as well as a religious motive behind the King's action. Looked at in this light, it may be that this abbey deserved its fate, though not, perhaps, the ruthless destruction that followed upon its dissolution. (But then, what are you to do with a host of magnificent buildings when there is no one to live in them?) The men that built this abbey built in love and awe and wonder. But they were succeeded by abbots who were more worldly, too worldly, and who by their scheming helped to bring about the downfall not only of this abbey but also that of religious institutions of the same kind throughout the country. The Cistercian Order arose during a period of earnest religious revival, as a protest against the laxity (and worse) that ruled in Benedictine and Cluniac houses. The Cistercian rule was austere. The meanest and coarsest of garb, a rough white woollen garment, had to be worn by the monks for work during the day, and the same garment had also to serve as night-gown. The rule of silence was strictly enforced, and everything was very simple. The new order had a most marked effect in raising the standard of living, both in the spiritual and in the material sense, in the monasteries of the twelfth and thirteenth centuries. But it also contained one great weakness, a weakness inherent in its inspiration and one which had become most marked by the time of Henry VIII. It was alien to the organization of the Church in this country. It gave no allegiance to the bishops, owing allegiance only to the parent abbey at Citeaux. This gave to ambitious, politically-minded, abbots—and a surprising number of them were both—enormous scope for scheming. Such men inevitably became a source of disunion in the national Church and so something of a danger to the nation itself. Certainly the Cistercian houses provided Henry VIII with the excuse for which he was looking, and certainly the Cistercian houses were dealt with rather more ruthlessly than most.

So now we look at a ruin. But the splendid dignity of the original abbey may be judged by the few remaining arches, by the lay brothers' dormitory, and by the monks' refectory, which is now the parish church. This church is, I think, unique in Britain in that its orientation is not east and west, but north and south. It was, of course, never intended to be a church. It was the monks' dining-room, built in accordance with the normal Cistercian practice standing north and south. And, in accordance with their austere rule, it was necessarily a cheerless room. But it has been most beautifully fitted-up and it makes a most beautiful church. Particularly noteworthy is the singularly beautiful Early English pulpit on the west side, a remarkably fine example of the work of the first half of the thirteenth century. Originally, of course, it was not a pulpit, but the rostrum from which one monk read some uplifting homily the while his brothers chewed a frugal meal in silence. It is approached by a stone stairway actually built within the thick wall. There are eighteen steps of uneven height, worn by the passage of many feet through a matter of seven hundred years, and the monks as they climbed them were visible all the way (as is the preacher today) through an arcade of moulded arches.

But there is no need to describe Beaulieu Abbey in detail. The details are to be found in a really excellent guide, which is on sale at the gate. The money goes towards the upkeep of the place. No one who has walked round Beaulieu Abbey and drunk of its peace and drawn of its inspiration can possibly think the money for this guide money wasted.

For this is a really beautifully kept ruin. The second Lord Montagu of Beaulieu, a man of immense versatility and an outstanding and much loved landlord, spent his life in preserving and beautifying his home and making it intelligible to visitors. It was he who restored the lay brothers' dormitory, which is now used as a meeting-place and is one of the most beautiful rooms in the country. It was he who rebuilt the Chapter-house arches and started the Abbey museum, which contains many treasures excavated from the ruins. He lies in a secluded corner of the cloisters, a fitting resting-place for one who loved his home so well, who thought always of what he could do for his property, not of what it might be made to do for him.

The present Lord Montagu carries on the tradition. But it is more difficult now and he has been forced, as have so many in like situation, into the "entertainment business". But, as one would expect from the setting and the tradition, here there is dignity. It was as a tribute to the fame of his father as a pioneer motorist that the present holder of the title founded the Montagu Motor Museum. This remarkable collection of veteran cars and motor-cycles, ancient fire-engines and so forth (and a no less remarkable collection of ancient pedal-cycles) is beautifully kept and exceptionally well displayed and documented, and attracts, along with the Abbey ruins and the Palace House, a quarter of a million or more visitors a year, who thus help to maintain the beauty of this most beautiful place.

Lower down the river is Buckler's Hard. This was once a famous place. In the days of Adams, the shipbuilder, Buckler's Hard held its head high among the shipbuilding yards of England. Here they built, from Forest oaks, great ships: *Illustrious* of seventy-four guns; *Agamemnon*, *Europe*, *Indefatigable* and *Vigilant* of fifty-four guns; *Euryalus* and *Greenwich*, *Sheerness* and *Swiftsure*, of forty-four. Of these, *Agamemnon*, *Euryalus*, *Illustrious* and *Swiftsure* fought at the Battle of Trafalgar. The slipway from which these great men-of-war were launched is still here. As you look at it, and the narrow winding stream beyond, it seems incredible that such ships could have been built here; utterly incredible that, having been built, they could ever have reached the open sea. Yet they were and did. They were towed down the winding stream by men in row-boats—and that could have been no easy task, for the fairway twists and turns in every direction and a large spit of shingle and mud stretches out from Needs Oar Point (most aptly named!) at the mouth—and then towed, still by men in row-boats, all the way round to Portsmouth. The thought takes the breath away.

Buckler's Hard today is just what it has always been; just one street, a broad street with grass verges running down a gentle hill to the blue waters of the Beaulieu River—and beyond the wooded shore by Exbury and the gulls flashing white against the green, their screams the only sound to break the stillness. At the foot of the hill, hard by the water, is the master-builder's house, an eighteenth-century building, which was converted—and, as one would expect, beautifully converted—under the direction of the second Lord Montagu of Beaulieu into a modern hotel by his estate craftsmen. The street is lined on each side by ten cottages, built of that delightfully rich brick that was made when Anne was Queen, with leaded lights and green or brown mullions and transoms. One of these cottages—on the left as you go towards the river—is a chapel: just one small room, but so simply beautiful that one is reluctant to leave. From each cottage there runs a neat stone-bordered path across the grass verge to the broad street. Neat: neat is the word that best describes Buckler's Hard. The little place is neat and tidy: ship-shape.

From Buckler's Hard a lane leads to the great barn at St Leonards and from there a pleasant, little-used road runs to Lymington. But for most people it will probably be better to return to Beaulieu, take the Brockenhurst road and then, at Hatchet Gate, the left fork for Lymington. The road runs past Hatchet Pond, quite a fair-sized sheet of water, and over Beaulieu Heath. There used to be a number of Round Barrows on Beaulieu Heath, but they were destroyed in 1941 to make way for a large airfield. Beaulieu Heath has a truly moorland aspect, barren and wind-swept, and gives the impression of being high ground, although, in fact, it is only a little over a hundred feet above sea-level at its highest point. From here you can look across to the low line of the Isle of Wight, only seven miles away as the crow flies, but seemingly many, many times that distance. On a fine day with the sun lighting the chalk cliffs where The Needles thrust boldly into the sea there are few more satisfying views in all England.

Lymington lies outside the Forest boundary. But it is essentially a Forest town. It lay within the Conqueror's New Forest and to this day all its links are with the Forest. It is the chief shopping centre for those who live in the southern part of the Forest and, if you would go to the Isle of Wight by the Lymington ferry (by far the most beautiful crossing) then, you must first pass through the Forest.

Lymington is very old—as we have seen the Iron Age Celts were here, the Romans certainly had a station here (some historians believe that the Lymington River is the "Rivar Alanius" where the Roman General Aulus Platius landed in A.D. 43), and "ton" is a Saxon affix—and is mentioned in Domesday Book, when it was a small cluster of cottages at the water's edge. Its charter as a borough dates from 1150, which gives it a longer borough history than Poole and makes it, in fact, the oldest borough in Hampshire, older by five years than Winchester, the ancient capital of England. And that is a history of which it may well be proud.

Like all ancient boroughs Lymington has had its ups and downs. Once it was an important port—it supplied twice as many ships as Portsmouth for the invasion of France in 1345—important enough to be attacked and burnt three times by the French. And once it was a very important salt-mining town. As late as the middle of the eighteenth century it paid as much as £60,000 a year in duty; in those days a very considerable sum. The salt pans, or salterns, were worked out by 1845 and the industry ceased. Lymington had a long period when life was pretty hard, when prosperity passed it by. Today it is once again a prosperous town with a number of light industries and one factory, Wellworthy's, whose products (pistons, piston rings, power-handling compressors, and so forth) are exported all over the world. And the yachtsmen—it is now very "U" to own a boat—bring money into the town, particularly, of course, in summer.

Though so ancient a place, there is little in modern Lymington that is really old. The parish church was originally built in 1250 and has a pleasant Early English chancel. The tower was built in 1670 and the cupola is Georgian. Architecturally, having regard o the long history of the town, this is a rather disappointing church. Indeed, I suppose that architecturally Lymington as a whole is disappointing—but then, one must remember that the French were prone to burn it—though there are some good Georgian houses. Architecturally it may be disappointing, but the wide main street with, at its seaward end, the sudden drop of Quay Hill is one of the most attractive in England.

The oldest church in the borough is that of All Saints at Milford-on-Sea. (Most people, of course, do not regard Milford-on-Sea as being part of Lymington. In fact, since 1932 the Borough of Lymington has included Milford-on-Sea, New Milton, Barton-on-Sea, Hordle and Pennington.) This is one of the very few churches in Hampshire mentioned in the Domesday Book, but it is not a pre-Conquest church. The original Norman church consisted of a short nave with side aisles and a small chancel. Two of the original Norman arches still stand in the south arcade of the western portion of the nave and the small south doorway of the transept is also Norman, though what its original purpose was cannot now be determined. For the rest, the church is mainly Early English. The tower, which was built in the early part of the thirteenth century, is of two stages and is quite exceptional among English church towers in that it has two "lean-to" adjuncts on the north and south which prolong the Norman aisles. These form little annexes, each lighted by a small lancet window, and they open into the tower through low-pointed arches. The octagonal spire was probably added in the fourteenth century. About the middle of the thirteenth century a considerable enlargement was made on the east side when the long chancel was added and a bay added to the nave. It is difficult to understand why this should have been done. Milford, at this time and for centuries afterwards, was no more than a very small village. The enlargement could not have been made necessary by the demands of a greatly increased congregation. Perhaps a clue is to be found in the windows of this part of the church. They are exceptionally good examples of the beginning of tracery. Can it be that a budding master-builder lived in this village and tried his hand out here before moving to some greater work?

From Milford you get an excellent view of Hurst Castle, lonely and grim in solitary grandeur on the shingle spit which extends south-eastwards into the Solent. It was to Hurst Castle that Charles I was brought on the first stage of his journey from Carisbrooke Castle to the block in Whitehall. Here he was lodged (the polite euphemism for "imprisoned") from 30 November to 16 December 1648. He might, just possibly, have escaped from Carisbrooke Castle—and perhaps Cromwell would have been relieved had he done so, but he was there for more than a year and made no attempt to do so—there could be no escape from Hurst Castle and there could be no attempt at rescue. The King must have known, I think, that his fate had been decided, that any trial there might be would be a farce, the verdict prejudged, when he was removed to this isolated fortress.

At the beginning of the nineteenth century, when England lived under the threat of invasion by Napoleon, considerable alterations were carried out and the castle, which had fallen into disrepair (though still garrisoned) was greatly strengthened. In 1873 new wings were built to the east and west, which partly conceal the original Tudor castle, and the interior was completely redesigned. A small garrison was maintained until 1933, when the castle was handed over to the then Office of Works as an ancient monument. However, it was again garrisoned by the army during the second World War.

Hurst Castle is open to the public daily, including Sundays, though the hours of opening vary according to the season of the year. You can reach it by the ferry from Keyhaven during the summer months or you can walk along the shingle bank from Milford-on-Sea. I do not recommend this walk in winter. It is hard enough in summer—two stiff miles of shingle, and shingle does not make for easy walking—but it is a good walk then, for it does bring home the grim isolation of the place with only the gulls and their wailing for company.

Returning to Lymington town, take the Brockenhurst road. In a mile or so you are back within the boundary of the New Forest and at the village of Boldre. This is a village without plan, for it spreads here, there, and everywhere—it is, indeed, a parish rather than a village—the cottages stretching out along wooded lanes

A Roebuck in Little Linford Inclosure
A Sika stag at wallow

without regard to a village centre. Boldre has something of a reputation as a beautiful village. I think "quaint"—quaint in the modern meaning of the word—would be a better description. The thatched cottages should be truly beautiful, but somehow they only succeed in being quaint. There is a bit too much of "ye olde" about Boldre for my taste. But Boldre has a nice church, an entrancing mixture of Norman and Early English, though without any outstanding features. And Boldre had an outstanding vicar in William Gilpin.

Gilpin ministered here for thirty years—there is a mural monument to his memory in the north aisle which was erected by the parishioners, a tribute earned by remarkably few vicars in English village history and one which speaks volumes for the regard in which he must have been generally held—and it was here that he wrote *Forest Scenery*. Gilpin was a contemporary of Gilbert White, but his literary efforts are not nearly so well known; largely, I think, because his style is not so simple. Certainly he knew a good deal about natural history, and he might, had he had the good fortune to meet Pennant, have done for the New Forest what Gilbert White did for Selborne. Gilpin did a great deal for Boldre and there can be no doubt that he was exceptionally popular with his parishioners. When he came to Boldre he found the village "utterly neglected by the former pastor, and, exposed to every temptation of pillage and robbery from their proximity to the deer, the game, and the fuel of the forest, these poor people were little better than a herd of banditti". He soon put a stop to that. But he did not confine his attentions to the poor. He was not, as are so many pillars of the Church, afraid to tackle the rich. It is on record that a wealthy farmer in the neighbourhood, who had a considerable fame as a lady-killer, was taken to task on many occasions by the worthy Mr Gilpin. These warnings had no effect, and finally the vicar banned him in the spiritual court. Sentence of excommunication was suspended only on condition that he performed penance in public. This he and his latest lady friend, clad in the white sheets that were the recognized penitential garments, duly did in the presence of a large congregation (news of the "ceremony" had spread and people came from far and wide

9

Mad March hares
Fox cubs waiting for mother

to witness it) and thereafter lived in peace with the vicar. In those days the Church had power and commanded respect. Nevertheless, it is evident that William Gilpin, in addition to being an author and a naturalist of no mean ability, was a man of very strong personality. He deserved, I think, a greater fame than has fallen to his lot.

His, however, is not the only literary connection that Boldre can boast. Warner, who wrote *Collections for the History of Hampshire* —five volumes of them!—was curate here. And Southey was married in Boldre church in 1839 to his second wife, Caroline Bowles, also an author. Southey's fame must surely be based on the quantity rather than the quality of his writings. No one now reads Caroline Bowles. Yet her *Chapters on Churchyards* has a charm which no book of her husband's ever attained.

Two miles north of Boldre lies Brockenhurst, a village of about the same size as Lyndhurst, but with the great advantage of a railway station, which is also the junction for Lymington and the ferry to the Isle of Wight, on the main London–Bournemouth line. The railway has made Brockenhurst the chief residential centre of the New Forest.

Within the parish boundary lies some of the best woodland scenery in the New Forest, though Brockenhurst itself is not particularly beautiful. The church (St Nicholas) is, however, interesting. Standing, like so many Forest churches, on a knoll, it has a well-wooded churchyard which includes some fine forest trees and a magnificent yew and it has the distinction of being the only remaining church within the boundaries of the present New Forest mentioned in Domesday Book. The nave and the south door (which is a good example of the work of the period) are Norman and there is a fine Norman font of Purbeck marble. The charming tower and spire are eighteenth century.

In the churchyard lies a great New Forest character, Brusher Mills; so-called because of the careful way in which he would sweep the pitch of the cricket ground on Balmer Lawn between innings. The headstone bears a carving of snakes and a hut among trees. Brusher Mills was a professional snake-catcher. He would pick up adders with his bare hands—he used to keep them in an old dustbin until he had enough to sell—and it is said that he was never bitten because he drank a bottle of rum a day and never washed! The carving of the hut among trees commemorates a sad, but true story. There was—maybe there still is—an old forest law which gave a man the right to claim a piece of land if he fenced it and lived on it for thirty years without interference. Brusher Mills fenced a little piece of ground in the heart of a wood, built himself a ramshackle hut, and lived there without interference for all but thirty years. But on the day before that little piece of ground would have been his, he drank a little too much and his tongue wagged. Someone went and pulled the fence down and wrecked the hut. Mills went back to find his home gone. The incident broke the old man's heart and he died a fortnight later.

The road runs north from Brockenhurst, as straight as the flight of an arrow and through some magnificent woodland scenery, to Lyndhurst. We are back where we began.

VI

THE NEW FOREST: FAUNA

ALTHOUGH there are many more cattle than ponies in the Forest, it is the ponies that invariably attract the attention of the visitor. They are by far the best known of all the Forest animals; and its greatest tourist amenity.

Ponies have been in the Forest from time immemorial. "Wild horses" are mentioned as being in the New Forest in the *Constitutiones de Foresta*, an early Norman Forest Code, which is sometimes, erroneously, ascribed to King Canute. It is beyond question that there was originally a breed of small horses native to these islands and it is tempting to think (quite a lot of people succumb to this temptation!) that all our modern mountain and moorland pony breeds derive from that ancient stock and bear some resemblance to it. But if that distinction can be claimed by any of our modern breeds, the New Forest pony certainly is not one of them. Probably only the Exmoor—the Shetland is, surely, of a different ancestral stock—bears any resemblance to the original native breed, for it has been but little subject to out-crossing and possesses to this day certain dominant characteristics; for example, the mealy nose. What little foreign blood was introduced into the Exmoor (and there was very little) never had any marked effect and has long since been absorbed. This has not been the case with the New Forest pony. There have been endless attempts to "improve" the breed: so many and over so long a period that no one today can have the least idea what the New Forest pony of, say, two hundred years ago looked like.

It is known that Queen Victoria lent a grey Arab stallion, Zorah, to the Verderers and that he stood at New Park from 1852 to 1860. Many people think that this was the first attempt at "improvement", but Zorah was certainly not the first Arab stallion to stand in the Forest. There must have been many such outcrosses before because, to this day, a markedly eastern type occasionally reappears.

In 1891 the Association for the Improvement of the Breed of New Forest Ponies was founded with the object of awarding annual prizes and premiums to stallions after they had been passed by the Verderers to run in the Forest. In 1893 Lord Arthur Cecil, believing that the best way of ensuring improvement was by introducing fresh blood of other mountain and moorland breeds, began importing stallions from Dartmoor, Exmoor, the Fells, the Highlands and Wales. In 1906 the Burley and District New Forest Pony and Cattle Society was formed and in 1910 this Society commenced publishing a Stud Book. For this purpose a New Forest pony was defined as being (a) one known to the Agisters as such and (b) one whose dam was a pony which has run on the Forest for at least one season as a three-year-old or upwards and whose sire was a pony stallion passed at Lyndhurst or by the Verderers or standing in the New Forest Parliamentary Division. This, it will be realized, was a very loose definition. Just how loose can be judged from the fact that at the Stallion Show in 1941 out of 121 ponies exhibited nine were Welsh, five were Dartmoor, four were Exmoor and four were Highland. At that time, and for many years afterwards, it can safely be said that the New Forest pony was a real mongrel. Moreover, the introduction of new blood was not always successful and there were many poor, weedy specimens in the Forest.

This policy stopped in 1938. I think that I am correct in saying that "foreign" blood has not been introduced since that date—at least, not into ponies running in the Forest—and since the best stallions are now retained by the granting of generous premiums and the Verderers' by-laws relating to the removal of scrub stallions of two years old and over from the Forest are strictly enforced, there has been a wonderful improvement in the overall standard of the breed. Indeed, considering the very mixed ancestry of the modern New Forest pony, it is remarkable how closely these ponies now conform to one type, and do so more closely year by year. Though their breeders would like to think that this is due solely to their own skill, this is, of course, not wholly true. What has happened is that, as man has stopped interfering with Nature by introducing "foreign" blood to "improve" the breed, Nature has been able to assimilate all the various types and so to produce the one most suited to the conditions in which it must live. One cannot improve upon Nature, though man invariably discovers this only after years of trial and error.

New Forest ponies come in any colour—occasionally one sees what is probably an ancestral type (for this colouring turns up in mountain and moorland ponies all over the world), dun with a dark dorsal stripe—but bays and browns are by far the most common. In height they vary between twelve and fourteen hands, have rather short necks, rather large heads (often with a distinctly eastern stamp) and drooping narrow quarters, but good strong shoulders and great depth through the heart.

Excluding animals turned out especially for the summer grazing (which may number a couple of hundred or so every year), there are probably rather more than a thousand ponies running the Forest throughout the year. These ponies may be divided into two groups, distinct by habit: those that habitually feed on the open Forest and those that habitually feed in the lanes and on the roadside verges. (The latter include many expert dustbin-openers!) Except in the breeding-season, the two groups do not mix. It is rare for a lane-feeder to take to the open Forest—those mares taken there by their stallions will invariably return with their foals at the earliest opportunity—and most uncommon for a forest-feeder to take to the lanes.

Though a drive through the Forest would not suggest this, the forest-feeders far outnumber the lane-feeders. They lead a wholly wild life and have the habits of genuinely wild animals. Unfortunately, this is not widely understood. Winter after winter one hears horrifying stories of "starving" ponies. There need never be any fear that ponies in the New Forest, even in the most bitter of winters, will die of starvation. In really bitter weather food is put out for them by the Pony Society and by the R.S.P.C.A. In a normal winter there is always plenty of food available: brambles, gorse, heather, holly. This may not be the sort of food that the town-dweller may consider suitable, but it is, in fact, excellent food. The New Forest pony is an exceptionally hardy animal, very well able to look after itself, its wits sharpened by the constant struggle for existence, a tough and excellent example of the wisdom of Nature's law "the survival of the fittest". The few that may die in a really bitter winter are also, of course, excellent examples of the wisdom of that law.

It is often thought that the ponies wander at will throughout the Forest. It is true that there is nothing to stop them doing so, but, in fact, the mares keep within fairly restricted territories. A mare, turned out for the summer grazing, can usually be found within something like a half-mile radius of the point of release. Mares on the Forest throughout the year naturally have a somewhat larger territory than this—and, of course, a larger territory in winter than in summer—nevertheless they do not travel nearly as far as one might imagine. On the other hand, stallions, in the breeding season, may travel considerable distances in search of mares. Each stallion gathers unto himself a small herd of mares and guards them in very much the same manner as a stag does his hinds.

There are four species of deer in the Forest: fallow, red, roe, and sika. The red deer, the indigenous deer of the Forest, the deer that the Normans loved to hunt, is now very scarce. It has been estimated that there are today no more than a score in the Forest and that all of these are confined to the area south-east of the railway. Why this should be so—if, indeed, it is so—is not understood.

Though not plentiful, red deer were certainly not uncommon in the Forest north-west of the railway up to the outbreak of the first World War. They were then present in small numbers in Oakley Inclosure and in rather larger numbers in Holly Hatch, Milkham, and Slufters, all inclosures to the north of the Ringwood–Cadnam road. They suffered very badly, mainly from poachers, during the first World War. After that war there were very few left in the northern part of the Forest. But there were a few: at least up to 1937 when the Buckhounds found a seventeen-pointer near Fritham and killed him near Whiteparish, well beyond the Forest boundary. From that date until 1949 there appears to be no record of red deer north of the railway. In 1949 a good stag was seen in the Godshill area (in the extreme north-west of the Forest) and this animal—at least, it was presumed to be the same one—lived in this area and was seen on many occasions until 1957, when it was observed to be injured and was shot. It is strange that there should be, throughout this period 1949–57, no record of red deer hinds in this area. Celibacy has no place in Nature. In fact, there were red deer hinds north of the Ringwood–Cadnam road during this period. Kenneth Whitehead records, in his *The Deer of Great Britain and Ireland*, that two were seen on open heath near Buckherd Bottom in 1951. It would thus seem probable that there were a few red deer, not just one stag, in the northern part of the Forest throughout this period. But it must be admitted that there are no records of their occurrence in this part of the Forest between 1957, when the Godshill stag was shot, and 1962. (This is not to say that there were no red deer in the area during this time: most people are content to recognize a deer, few bother about the species.) In 1962 a number of red deer escaped from a small park near Ringwood and some were seen in the Forest north of the Ringwood–Cadnam road from time to time until the end of 1963. I know of no report of them since then. On the other hand, I know of no report of them being killed. I think it possible, probable even, that there are still a few red deer in the northern part of the Forest.

Beyond this possibility the red deer are confined to the area south-east of the railway. It might be thought from this that the railway constitutes a barrier against northward spread. But this, of course, is not so. The red deer of the Surrey-Sussex-Hampshire borders think nothing of crossing electrified railway lines. The red deer of the south-eastern part of the Forest do not cross the railway —but are we sure that they never do so?—simply because, with their small numbers (the total population is estimated at about a score), there is plenty of room for them south-east of the line. What is difficult to understand is why the numbers are so small.

It is true that they suffered severely during the second World War, at the end of which it was thought that there were no more than half-a-dozen left. But that is a long time ago now. They are not hunted nor are they shot. One would, therefore, have expected a greater increase in numbers than there has been. The red deer of the New Forest certainly pose some intriguing problems.

In 1904 a pair of Japanese sika kept by Lord Montagu of Beaulieu escaped. In 1905 he released another pair to keep them company. These four gave rise to a population which, between the wars, probably reached a total in excess of two hundred. As they did very considerable damage to the forestry plantations, to young conifers in particular, their numbers were drastically reduced and are now strictly controlled. The present population is estimated at about sixty head. All of these are south-east of the railway: I know of no record of any sika north of the line. But, again, this does not mean that the railway acts as a barrier to northward spread. It merely indicates that the sika are, at present, in no need of *lebensraum*. Were the population allowed to increase normally the railway would certainly prove no barrier. Deer are not so easily confined! In any case it will not, I fancy, be long before there are some sika in the northern part of the Forest. There are already a few in the woods around Romsey and there has been some spread northwards (across railway lines!) from the considerable population centred on the Purbeck heathlands.

Roe deer are now widespread, though not really plentiful. Indigenous to Britain, the roe became extinct in the southern counties —or so it was believed; there must once have been a considerable number in the Forest, for the wood between Buckherd Bottom and the Linford Brook is called Roe Wood—and was reintroduced into Dorset early in the nineteenth century. The first roe deer recorded in the Forest after the Dorset reintroduction was in 1880 and the spread thereafter was very slow. Indeed, it was not until after the first World War that the roe really settled down and began to spread. It has been doing so ever since. It now occurs throughout the Forest, being most numerous on Holmesley Walk and Wilverley, least numerous in the south-east corner beyond the Beaulieu River. The roe deer are not hunted by the Buckhounds, but they are "controlled" and a number are shot annually by the keepers. The present population is estimated at about three hundred and fifty. This is likely to be an under- rather than an over-estimate.

The common deer of the Forest is the fallow. There is considerable doubt as to whether the fallow deer we know today is indigenous or was introduced. It is known that there were fallow deer in Britain during the last inter-glacial period, but it is thought that these disappeared during the last Ice Age and that the deer we know today were introduced at a later period: some authorities suggest by the Phoenicians, some by the Romans. I must say I think it very unlikely that the Phoenicians, a Mediterranean people who engaged in the tin trade with Cornwall but who, so far as is known, made no permanent settlements here, would have bothered to bring fallow deer with them. There could not possibly have been a trade in fallow deer with Bronze Age Britain and no merchant would be likely to clutter up his deck with deer when the space could be more profitably filled. I think that introduction by the Phoenicians can be dismissed straightaway. And I must say that I am not very impressed by the Roman theory. The Romans came as soldiers and administrators rather than as settlers. Probably every Roman official hoped that he would be back in a warmer climate within a year or so. The "top brass" might have brought pheasants with them, but surely not deer. I find the theory advanced by Richard Glover in Kenneth Whitehead's *The Deer of Great Britain and Ireland*, that the fallow deer were introduced by the Gauls—that is, the Belgae, the last wave of Iron Age Celts, some of whose princes ruled on both sides of the Channel— much more acceptable.

This is all rather academic. It is mentioned here only because you will still hear some authorities speaking of the fallow deer as a "feral" animal, which seems to me to be taking pedantry to its ultimate lengths. One might also deny the genuine wildness of the rabbit (introduced by the Normans) and the pheasant. Accepting that the fallow deer is an introduced species, it has still been here for around two thousand years and for almost the whole of that time, if not for the whole of it, some (and more and more year by year) have been leading a truly wild existence. One of the most difficult things is to keep deer in a deer park. We with all our modern aids find it difficult enough. The Iron Age Celts or the Romans (and it is so long ago now that it really does not matter which), if they did have deer parks—and there is, so far as I am aware, absolutely no evidence that they did—would have found it very much more difficult. There must have been escapes from the very beginning. The fallow deer has been a wild animal in Britain for so long now, that we might as well forget that it was ever introduced and accept it for what it is: a genuinely wild and very successful wild animal.

We do not know how many fallow deer there were in the Forest in Norman times, but the protection they then received must, of course, have brought about a great increase in their numbers and they went on increasing steadily at least until Stuart times. A census taken in 1670 gave an estimated population of seven and a half thousand; almost certainly an under-estimate. This, say eight thousand, would seem to have been the peak population attained by fallow deer in the Forest. From that time on there was a gradual, but steady, decrease in numbers. This would not have been because many more were killed each year (though undoubtedly many more were), but because the population had increased beyond that which the available food supply could support. A census taken towards the end of the eighteenth century gave an estimated population of six thousand and another, taken in 1830, one of just over five thousand. At the time of the Deer Removal Act (1851) the number of fallow deer in the Forest was estimated at about four thousand; again, probably an under-estimate. Under that Act all the deer were not removed, but there was a very considerable slaughter, and of course, the disturbance caused many deer to migrate to quieter places on the fringes of the Forest. But they soon began to increase again and by 1877 were again becoming something of a nuisance. From that time onwards an annual toll was taken. A certain number were shot each year and they were also hunted, which, if it did not cause the death of a significant number, did cause some disturbance; in itself a not ineffective method of control. In 1892 Lascelles estimated—he would not have found a Commoner to agree with him!—the population of fallow deer in the Forest at two hundred and fifty. Though this was certainly an under-estimate, there can be no doubt that numbers had been drastically reduced and that, during his reign, control was both strict and effective.

After the retirement of Lascelles there was, particularly in the years immediately prior to the first World War, some increase in numbers and there was certainly an increase between the wars. I have no figures for this period, but, living in the Forest, one could not but be aware of it: you saw more deer. Moreover, between the wars, and particularly in the thirties, the annual kill of the Buckhounds was a good deal higher than it had been previously. The second World War, with the great disturbance it brought to the Forest, naturally caused a sharp fall in numbers. In 1949 Mr Oliver Hook estimated the population at about four hundred and fifty. Despite the annual (and increasing) toll taken by the keepers, despite the activities of the Buckhounds (and their total of kills is going up), the number has increased steadily since then and is now certainly in excess of a thousand.

There are four distinct colour varieties of fallow deer. The common variety in the Forest is chestnut with white spots in summer, the spots being lost in winter, when the coat turns to dark brown with a white belly. The variety known as "Menil", which is generally of a rather brighter chestnut and in which the spots are retained in winter, also occurs in the Forest, but is rare. I have, myself, never seen one. Also rare in the Forest is the black variety, in which there are no white spots in summer and in which the coat turns a sooty grey in winter. I have once seen a black fallow in the Forest; a solitary buck on the fringe of Puckpits Inclosure by Withybed Bottom in 1948. The fourth variety is known as "white", though it is actually cream-coloured. It is not an albino. A magnificent white buck frequented the Lucy Hill area for some four years just before the war and what may have been the same animal was reported from the same area in 1945. It would be wrong to describe this variety as common or even frequent, but there are certainly more white fallow in the Forest—

and have been for many years—than one would imagine from the occasional sight of one. Whitehead says that it was estimated that there were at least twenty-seven of this colour in the Forest in 1961: thirteen bucks of varying ages, eleven does, and three fawns.

Roe deer seem to be in some competition with the sika and the fallow in the Forest. It is in the area in which the sika are most common that the roe are uncommon. And in those woods in which the fallow live in considerable numbers, roe are unlikely to be plentiful. I do not know that there is any competition between fallow and sika: I think not.

I have noticed that the deer in the Forest avoid the cattle—if there are cattle grazing at the edge of a wood, you will be extremely unlikely to see deer—but they do not object to the ponies and fallow deer have even been seen to play with them. My friend Juliette de Bairacli Levy, in her *Wanderers in the New Forest*, records that Len Witt of Godshill has many times in dark and quiet places of the Forest "seen the ponies gambolling with the deer, leaping and prancing in happy company". I have not—and how I wish I had—seen anything like that. But I have seen a small party of fallow deer pass through a herd of ponies, and neither took the least notice of the other. And I have watched fallow feeding in close proximity to ponies, obviously completely undisturbed by their presence.

Mostly, of course, people see the deer at night in the headlights of the car. A particularly good place for this sort of view is the by-road which runs from Burley, passing between Oakley Inclosure on the one hand and Burley New Inclosure on the other and then between Anderwood Inclosure and Dames Slough Inclosure, to join the main Lyndhurst–Bournemouth road. There have been very few occasions, at any season of the year, on which I have driven this road at night without catching deer in my headlights.

Apart from these accidental glimpses at night, the deer—the fallow and the sika at any rate; roe deer, in my experience, are much more unpredictable—are not really difficult to watch, provided that you know a little about their habits and take reasonable care. Evening, around dusk, is the best time, for it is then that they begin to emerge from the thick cover of the enclosures to feed in the rides or on the open lawns. This applies to both fallow and sika. The very early morning, up to about an hour after dawn, is just as good. But few, other than dedicated naturalists, are willing to get up as early as that! The best part of the Forest for the fallow deer is north of the Ringwood–Cadnam road. I have found Hawk-hill Inclosure and Perry Wood Inclosure, between Brockenhurst and Beaulieu, to be good for sika. The sika seem to lie up in dense cover throughout the daylight hours in both summer and winter: the fallow are much more inclined to move and feed during daylight hours in winter.

The fox is common and widespread throughout the Forest. In such country as this it poses some delicate problems. It is itself an efficient controller of small mammals—rats, mice, voles, moles, and the like—none of which are helpful to forestry at any time and some of which are liable to increase so rapidly in numbers in certain years (for example, years of abundant beechmast) that they may assume near-plague proportions. In such years the bank vole and the short-tailed vole particularly can do extensive damage to forestry plantations. The fox is, therefore, in no small measure the friend of the forester. It would be sound forestry practice, if not to encourage it, at least to do nothing about it. On the other hand, in such an area as the New Forest—and this to a much greater extent than in wholly agricultural districts (where greater care is taken)—the fox can be a considerable nuisance to its human neighbours and may sometimes cause considerable financial loss to poultry keepers. The Forestry Commission, therefore, destroy a good many, cubs particularly, as part of a "good neighbour" policy. Others are destroyed by the Hunt (the New Forest Foxhounds) and others in a number of other ways. There is, however, not the slightest risk that the fox, an animal exceptionally well able to take care of itself, will ever be seriously affected by these necessary control measures.

The badger is also widely distributed in the Forest. It would perhaps be an exaggeration to describe it as common, but it is certainly much more plentiful than is generally realized. This is understandable since it is almost wholly nocturnal in its habits. The sets—nearly always in little-frequented places in broad-leaved enclosures; I do not, personally, know of one in a conifer plantation—are, however, not too difficult to find because the badger treads well-worn paths through the undergrowth. Approach to a badger's set must always be made up-wind and as silently as possible. As with the deer and the fox, the badger, though less frequently, may be caught in the headlights of the car at night.

Otters, I am assured, occur from time to time on all the streams of the Forest; and I am sure that this is so. But seeing an otter is a matter of being in the right place at the right time; a matter of luck. I think you will be very lucky if you see an otter. And this applies also to stoat and weasel, both present in some numbers and both good friends of the forester. Both are so small and so quick in movement that it is not so much a matter of watching as of catching a glimpse.

Hares, animals usually associated with rolling downland and arable farmland, are (rather surprisingly perhaps) if not common, at least plentiful and widely distributed throughout the Forest. It is true that there are certain areas where they seem never to occur; but there are others where you may be fairly sure of seeing one or more on almost every visit. Their numbers are controlled to some extent by the New Forest Beagles—and, of course, a number are shot and, no doubt, a few are snared—but the hare, like the fox, is an animal very well able to take care of itself and, at least so far as the Beagles are concerned, it is helped to do so by the character of the country in which it lives.

When I was a boy, and up to the outbreak of the second World War and for a year or two afterwards, the squirrel of the Forest was the red squirrel. It was at one time present in such large numbers, indeed, that it had to be controlled to prevent excessive damage to young conifers. In 1909 disease pretty well decimated the red squirrel population in the Forest. There was subsequent recovery, of course, but the numbers never again attained the peak of 1908. Though they had become common again in the twenties control measures were stopped in 1927, sufficient indication that they were not present in sufficient numbers to constitute a menace to forestry. There was again some sort of epidemic disease in 1929, but by the late thirties the red squirrel was again common enough throughout the Forest, though their numbers were probably not then as great as they had been in 1929. In January 1940 the first grey squirrels appeared in the Forest—it may be presumed that they spread in from Bournemouth where there had long been a well-established colony—and now it is the grey squirrel that is the squirrel of the Forest. The red squirrel has, indeed, vanished.

Why this should be so no one really knows. The grey squirrel did not—as so many people, putting two and two together, not unnaturally think—attack and kill the red. Though the grey squirrel first invaded the Forest in 1940, it did not really become established in any considerable numbers before 1945 and by that time the red squirrel was already becoming scarce everywhere in the Forest. There were red squirrels around my family's home and in the garden at Burley in 1944 and there seemed then to be just as many as usual. And they were still there in 1945. Looking back from this distance of time it seems evident that there must have been many fewer. But that was certainly not apparent at the time. There were red squirrels about just as usual and one saw them frequently, and that was all that mattered: one did not bother to count them. As far as I can remember now, there were not many grey squirrels in Burley at that time. But in 1946 there were very few red squirrels in the village and by 1947 they had disappeared altogether, though one pair did hang on in Oakley Inclosure until 1949, but did not apparently breed successfully. That was the picture throughout the Forest. In 1949 it was estimated that there were no more than forty red squirrels in the whole of the Forest and very few young were raised. Now they have all gone.

The true explanation for the complete disappearance from the Forest of the red squirrel is probably much more complex than this; but it would seem that the arrival of the grey coincided with a period of decline in the red. There had been such periods of decline before—I have mentioned two, those of 1909 and 1929—

White Fallow buck

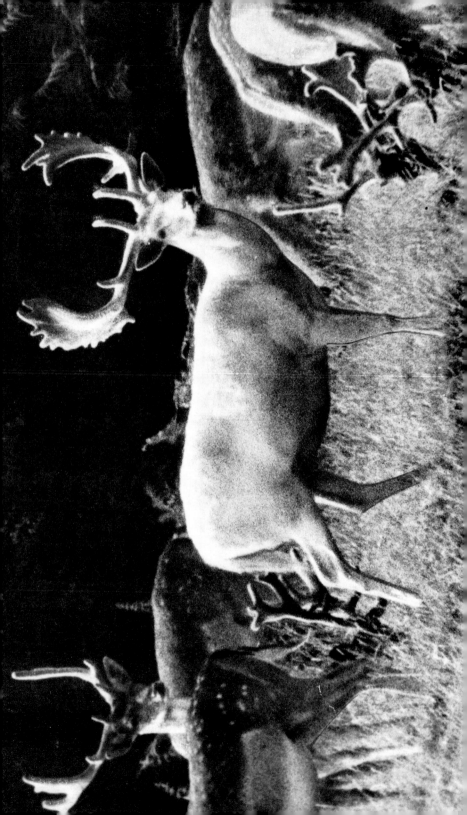

but each time the red squirrel had been able to make a good, if
not a complete, recovery, because it had no competition to face.
This time there was competition. The red squirrel, weakened by
disease and in insufficient numbers, was quite unable to hold its
own with the larger and more assertive grey squirrel in the vital
competition for food and was, therefore, unable to breed sufficiently freely to ensure survival.

So now we have the grey squirrel. Larger, hungrier, altogether
better fitted for the battle of life, the grey squirrel has this additional advantage: it is an introduced species and has no natural
enemies of any importance in this country. Man is its only enemy.
In the Forest thousands (literally thousands) are destroyed every
year. The slaughter, a most necessary slaughter, seems to have no
noticeable effect on the numbers of a real pest.

So far as birds are concerned, the New Forest, except for its
shoreline, must be described as disappointing. That remark, in
view of the fact that Edwin Cohen in his contribution to the
symposium, *The New Forest*, lists no fewer than 151 species, "of
which there is a reasonable chance of seeing some 133 at one
season or another", requires some explanation. I do not question
the figures; as one would expect from such an authority, they are
absolutely accurate. The New Forest, for the bird-lover living
within its borders or on the fringe of them, is certainly not disappointing. But for the visiting bird-lover? Except on the shoreline
(particularly in winter) what he will see—certainly around the
villages and the hotels—are the normal garden birds: the tits and
the finches, the blackbirds and the sparrows, and so on. The point
needs to be made to prevent disappointment. So many bird-lovers,
as distinct from ornithologists, so many people who have developed a genuine love of birds through feeding their garden birds at
the bird-table, are convinced that in wild country, in an area such as
the New Forest containing many acres of uninhabited and undisturbed land, they are bound to see a greater number and a
greater variety of birds. In fact, the reverse is the case. Except for
the inner suburbs of towns, the more cultivated land, the more
gardens, the more birds and in greater variety. The reason for this
is quite simple: the more cultivated land, the more gardens, the
10

A Forestry Commission badger gate in use

more hedgerows and shrubberies, the more bird-tables, the more food and the greater the number and variety of nesting sites. I expect to see, and do see, a greater variety of birds in my garden on the Hampshire-Surrey border than ever I see in the course of a visit to the New Forest. If I lived in, had a garden in, the New Forest, the situation would be different. But I am writing for the visitor.

Of course, there are in the New Forest a number of birds, common enough in their proper habitat, which rarely come into gardens. Of course, there are unusual birds, even real rarities, which turn up from time to time. But the sight of such a bird requires luck: the luck to be in the right place at the right time. Such birds may be discounted. But there is one resident rarity.

This is the Dartford warbler; the only British warbler which does not migrate, which is with us all the year round. It does occur elsewhere, in small and isolated pockets, mostly on the borders of Hampshire, but its chief home is the open heather-and-gorse land of the Forest. I do not know what numbers there are today—it has never been numerous and it is always affected by severe winters (and we have had a very severe one recently)—but it is certainly present in greater numbers than anywhere else. The Dartford warbler is a charming little bird, but, except in the breeding season, and particularly when it is feeding its young, it is astonishingly difficult to see, so closely does it cling to cover. If you want to see a Dartford warbler, persuade someone who knows a locality they frequent to take you there—and hope for the best. I have been disappointed many more times than I have been fortunate.

Other birds of the open heaths are the wheatear, the skylark and the meadow pipit (both common), the stonechat and the whinchat. The stonechat—the "fuzz-topper" in local parlance—is easy to see because it has a fondness for perching in prominent places. It also draws attention to its presence by its harsh call-note. Altogether not an easy bird to miss!

Three birds of the night—there are plenty of owls, of course—must also be mentioned: the nightingale, the nightjar, and the woodlark. The nightingale is plentiful and its wonderful song can be heard all over the Forest, except (I think) in the heart of the enclosures. It is a bird of the fringes of the thick woodlands, a bird of coppices and thickets on the heathlands. It is also, of course, in suitable places, a bird of garden shrubberies. We always reckoned to have one pair (and in good years we might have two) in the garden at Burley. The nightingale, by the way, is also a singer by day; but by day, with so many other birds in full song, its song is often not recognized for what it is. This applies also to the woodlark, another singer by day and night. If you hear a skylark singing at night, then you have heard a woodlark! The songs are, in fact, not exactly alike—the woodlark's is much more mellow—but there is a strong family resemblance. In the Forest, a stronghold of the woodlark, the bird prefers the edges of woodland where they abut on heathland. The nightjar, on the other hand, is very definitely a bird of the dusk and the dark, silent and hardly ever seen in daylight. It is plentiful throughout the Forest, but is particularly a bird of the rides and glades in the woodlands.

You will find that there are fewer birds of fewer species in the conifer woods than in the broad-leaved woods. Lack of water is certainly one of the chief reasons for this, but there are also, of course, fewer convenient nesting-places in conifer woods. But quite a numer of species can be attracted to conifer woods, provided that they are not too dry and draughty, and I am always surprised that this is not done more frequently by the Forestry Commission.

Most birds are the friends of the forester. It is true that some are eaters and scatterers of seeds; that some destroy buds, some bark, some timber; that some kill other birds or take their eggs. But most of them also destroy vast numbers of insects: and most insects are enemies of the forester. Indeed, though a few (such as the stag-beetle and the dragonflies) are harmless, I can think of none that could truthfully be described as beneficial to the forester. On the other hand, I can think of no bird that is an enemy of the forester—the woodpigeon is a pest of agriculture, not of silviculture—while some (the nightjar is a notable example) are wholly beneficial.

On the whole, so it has always seemed to me, British foresters tend to be indifferent to birds and do not do as much as they might to encourage them. Food, water, and nesting-sites are the essentials. Food there is in plenty and water in the New Forest is never far away. But nesting-sites? Most of the busiest insect-eaters frequenting woodland nest in holes in trees and there ought not to be many such sites in a well-managed woodland. But nest-ing-boxes can be provided. In many continental forests this is done as a matter of course. Four boxes to the acre is about the right density, for they are unlikely all to be used in the same year, for conifer plantations. There is still much work to be done on the place of birds in the economics of forestry.

But it is the shoreline—Christchurch Harbour and Stanpit Marsh, and then from Keyhaven to Needs Oar Point (though the public is now excluded from Tanner's Lane eastwards)—that is really exciting. Autumn and spring, and the months between, are the best for shore birds. There was a time when, living nearby, I visited the shore regularly at these times over a period of some fifteen years. In that time I saw all the wading birds usual around our coasts and several which can be accounted uncommon, and one or two that are definitely rare. In fact, on the shore in winter, you never know what may turn up.

If you are not accustomed to watching waders, a word of warning. The great difficulty about the many small waders that frequent our coasts is how to distinguish one species from another. They are nearly all very much of a size; their habits are similar; their winter plumage at least is not dissimilar; many are only birds of passage from the far north; all have superlative powers of flight; and, with one or two exceptions, all are extremely wary and alert. Moreover, their inaccessibility makes it hard to study them intimately. We can climb a tree, we can scale a cliff, but we cannot walk on a mudflat. So most of the watching has to be done from a distance, when most of the unmistakable points of identification, which are stressed in the bird books, are not so unmistakable. Even a colour at a distance is most deceptive—colours on the shore are deceptive enough at the best of times because there is so much reflected light—and it is only in good light and with good glasses that one can distinguish the delicate pencilling of their plumage. To begin with, they all look very much the same: subdued browns and greys merging into each other, with occasional bold splashes of black or white or chestnut. They are, too, very much the same in form: legs as slender as is consistent with use and body, bill, and general shape in harmony with the legs. Indeed, I think it wise to begin with to ignore the points of detail stressed in so many of the bird books. For example, some bird books tell you that the sanderling can be distinguished from other small waders by the absence of the hind toe. This is perfectly true. But if you, even with powerful glasses, can pick out a sanderling from a mixed flock of small waders, none of which will be still for more than a moment or two, on wet sand at a distance of a quarter of a mile and say definitely that it is a sanderling (an eight-inch bird) because it lacks a hind toe less than an inch in length—well, I cannot. But as one becomes familiar with marsh or mudflat, so one becomes familiar with its birds. One begins to distinguish species from species almost unconsciously. The cry is different; the flight is different; one bobs, one struts: they have different personalities. Small differences, difficult to put down on paper, but for all that very real differences.

Of course, it is nice to know what you are looking at: and in time you do. But quite apart from identification there is a magic about bird-watching on the shore that warms even the coldest day. These are birds of bustle and wayward thought. With their elusiveness, their caprice, their swift flight, their wild musical cries and disciplined, patterned, manœuvres over the desolate shore, they are nothing but aerial spirits visible for fleeting moments.

Which waders are you most likely to see on the Forest shore? Well, almost for certain (but, of course, not all of them at the same time) redshank, ringed plover, oyster-catcher (all three breed here) curlew, whimbrel, turnstone, black-tailed godwit, bar-tailed godwit, dunlin, knot, sanderling, little stint, ruff, grey plover, spotted redshank, greenshank, common sandpiper and green sandpiper. That is a good enough list and of course, there is always the chance of a real rarity.

In addition, the common tern, the little tern, the black-headed gull and the shellduck breed along this shore. And the shellduck, a brilliantly plumaged bird, is worth many an afternoon's watching. For it is a bird of character and something of a comedian. Indeed, each individual shellduck is so strongly individual, so much a personality, that you soon come to recognize individual birds (though each is alike in colour and shape) by their posture, walk, and so forth. More even than that: so strong is each individual personality that before long you will find yourself fitting names to the birds; you will find yourself recognizing individual birds as surely as you would recognize your own friends in the street. But you can do this only in the breeding season: the season of courting, nesting, and rearing the young. When that season ends, so ends individuality: all shellduck then look alike, save for that indefinable distinction that distinguishes duck from drake.

In general, the domestic life of the shellduck is above reproach, which is more than I can say for any other duck that I have watched at all closely. In 90 per cent of shellducks duck and drake are faithful, even jealous consorts, sticking closely together and showing every sign of affection. But there are others. I have known occasional drakes who seemed to regard every duck on the shore as fair game. And I have known ducks who spend their time feeding and wandering about the shore, making passes at the drakes. All very human.

The nestlings, as soon as they are hatched, are taken to the water by their parents. Sometimes this involves quite a long walk, and the young are shepherded along most carefully by both parents, the duck leading the little procession and the drake bringing up the rear. Adult shellducks often stamp in the shallows or on wet sand to bring up worms, and this skill is taught to the young at a very early stage. It is quite definitely taught. You will see one parent and then the other do it and then call to the young to take the worm, and then stamp again, and in no time at all you will see the young shellducks trying it for themselves, though they are then much too young and too light to have much effect on the worms.

After a little preliminary training there comes a marked and most interesting change in the attitude of the parents to their young. You will often see a crowd of young, perhaps twenty or more, in the charge of one pair of adults, a duck and a drake, or two ducks, but never two drakes. What happens is this: a number of little families are joined together and left in the charge of one pair of adults. This pair will look after them all just as if they were, in fact, all their own children. The party is not always in charge of a duck and a drake—I have an idea that the drakes do not much care for the job!—but often in charge of two ducks, who will take on the job for, say, the morning and will be relieved by another pair for the afternoon. I have an idea that these are definite "governess" ducks, adult females who either not mated or have for one reason or another lost their eggs. The gathering together of these schools—for that is what they are, preparatory schools—is not a haphazard business. It is not a matter of several families joining up by accident and then their parents taking the opportunity to creep away, shelving their responsibility for a while. There is nothing of that nature. The young are handed over to the birds in charge for the time being by the parents, and there is a particular ceremonial for the purpose. This consists of bowing, so low that the bill almost touches the ground, and the other bird responds by doing the same thing. The bow is usually repeated twice, and then the parents off-duty depart and the other pair takes over. And when there is a change of guardianship—and there is always at least one change during the day—the ceremonial is repeated. You will have a lot of fun watching sheldduck.

Half a mile inland from the shore is Sowley Pond, a large stretch of water which has a road running along its southern edge. This is an enormous advantage for those who do not relish the undeniable rigours of shore-watching in winter; and it must be admitted that shore-watching in winter is a pursuit for the dedicated bird-lover. Sitting in a car, moving slowly along the road in a car, you can see almost all the water. And from autumn to spring this is a great haunt of waterfowl. Here you may watch great crested grebe and coot, and a great variety of duck: teal and mallard, wigeon, golden-eye, pochard, tufted, shoveler, pintail. You will not see them all at the same time, of course: but those eight are fairly regular in winter. And every now and again, especially in really severe weather, a real rarity turns up at Sowley Pond.

Did I say that, bird-wise, the New Forest is disappointing? I take that back.

VII

THE NEW FOREST: FLORA

To the average Englishman the word "forest" suggests extensive woodlands, dark, secretive, with quiet glades between tall trees. It so happens that the New Forest is extensively wooded and that some of these woods are dark and quiet: but that is a coincidence due to large-scale planting by the Forestry Commissioners. The word "forest" does not, strictly, mean "wooded country" —that is a modern connotation—but rather a "wilderness". (It is, I think, identical with the Welsh *gores*, meaning "waste ground", which has survived in the English tongue as gorse, which is essentially a growth of waste-land.) Certainly in Norman times, and down at least until Tudor times (as we have already seen), the word meant a large area of waste-land. And still today the New Forest is in general a land of fairly open character.

The New Forest has three distinct faces, which are the expression of three different soil formations. Firstly, there are the flat-topped gravel plateaux or sandy plains, which are infertile barren areas, supporting a few self-sown Scots pine and birch, and much gorse and heather and various hardy grasses. This is the genuine heathland. Secondly, there are seams of rich, well-drained, clays and loams, supporting fairly thick natural woodland composed mainly of beech, oak, holly, thorn and yew. Thirdly, there are fairly broad areas of low-lying, ill-drained marshland, supporting alder thickets, bog-moss, bracken, cotton grass, heath, sedge and willow.

The first type, the genuine heathland, occurs in widely separated parts of the Forest, but is to be seen at its best in the north.

Between the Downton–Cadnam road and the Ringwood–Cadnam road the country consists of a series of flat-topped parallel ridges—Deadman Hill, Hampton Ridge, Ibsley Common, Broomy Walk, Handy Cross—between which the little forest streams have carved deep valleys, the "seams" which have given rise, here and there, to areas of natural woodland. (You will find that the areas of natural woodland, throughout the Forest, are usually situated on slopes separating flat-topped plateaux.) But, in the south of the Forest, there is Beaulieu Heath, which has very much the same aspect as the flat-topped plateaux of the north and which supports similar vegetation (gorse and heather), but which is at a lower elevation and which is not a ridge, but a wide plain. Here the soil is not gravel, but sand with a little gravel and the streams have not carved deep valleys. Naturally most of the marshland is to be found in the low-lying parts of the Forest, but here and there (surprisingly frequently indeed) you will find waterlogging on the flat-topped plateaux areas and where this does occur it gives rise to bog, just as it does on the high moorlands of the north of England and Scotland and Wales.

In early times the Forest was much more heavily wooded than it is today. There were not then the great expanses of treeless heath. These now treeless heaths then supported great woods of birch, the oldest of all British forest trees, and along the streams there were large thickets of alder. There would also have been many willows, some ash, and a good deal of thorn; and on the slopes woods consisting largely of oak, yew and holly.

These are the woods which are now known as "natural woodlands" or "amenity woodlands". These are the woods which give beauty to the Forest and shelter to the animals: these are the woods beloved by visitor and tourist alike. There are about 5,000 acres of this natural woodland in the Forest. They are maintained by the Forestry Commission, partly by means of small enclosures to ensure natural regeneration—without enclosures natural seeding is a very hazardous process owing to the appetites of grazing animals—and partly by planting, because of their amenity value, because of the outcry that would certainly be raised if they were not: not on economic grounds. In such areas as the New Forest, the Forestry Commission is very conscious of public opinion.

The modern concentration on "softwoods" (conifers) for which there is every justification economically—and, remember, the Forestry Commission's first interest is economic: forestry is an industry like agriculture, equally concerned with the production of marketable crops—has, inevitably, altered the character and changed the face of the Forest in no small degree. Yet I feel sure that it would be true to say that the New Forest today contains more trees of different kinds and more trees of different ages than any other forest in Britain. And that, surely, is a tribute to skilful and far-sighted management.

Nevertheless, one tree, the birch, has, undeniably, suffered under this economic stress. There is plenty of birch in the Forest, particularly along the edges of new enclosures where it is used as a "nurse" for conifers, but there are no birch plantations, no big birch woods. The birch is undoubtedly a much neglected tree in modern British forestry. This is, perhaps, understandable since conifers will thrive on most of the sites suited to birch. What is, surely, not justifiable is the attitude of many British foresters who seem to regard the birch rather as a weed than as a commercial timber tree.

The birch is *the* native tree of the Forest. It is exceptionally hardy and grows very rapidly, though it never forms a trunk of great girth. It would be impossible to make out an economic case for some of the other hardwoods native to the Forest—alder and willow, for example (though both have their uses)—but the birch, in addition to being a tree of great beauty—the "Lady of the Woods" of the poets—has great economic possibilities. In Scandinavia, where it is grown close together in plantations to produce straight boles, it is a tree of great commercial importance, particularly in the plywood trade, and it is also of great commercial importance in Canada. In this country, because it has never been properly cultivated, it is considered of little account. The birch timber used in British industry (and a great deal is used) is imported, either in the log or in a manufactured state, from Canada and northern Europe. In these days, when Government after Government stresses the importance of exporting more and importing less, this seems on the face of it to be quite ridiculous. One would have thought that we could with a little silvicultural skill (and we have great silvicultural skill at our command) supply within a comparatively short space of time at least a fair proportion of our plywood requirements.

The Forest is a botanist's paradise, for each of its three faces—the heathland, the woodland, and the marshland—has its characteristic flora and each its rarities.

Let us consider the heathland first; most colourful in spring, when the ridges and plains are clothed in gold, and in autumn, when the dress is changed to purple. The gold is the gold of the gorse. There are three species: two of them, the common gorse (*Ulex europaeus*) and the dwarf gorse (*Ulex minor*) are common; the third, which is intermediate in size, is *Ulex galii* and, though not rare, is much less plentiful. There is an old saying, "when gorse is out of bloom kissing is out of fashion", which is a picturesque way of saying that gorse is never out of bloom. The truth of this is to be seen on the plateaux of the Forest; there is no month in the year when you may not find gorse in flower somewhere. But May is the month for the common gorse and July the month for the softer-spined (but do not take liberties!) dwarf gorse. The purple comes with the bell-heather (*Erica cinerea*) and cross-leaved heath (*Erica tetralix*) and, a little later, the ling (*Calluna vulgaris*) with its smaller, rather paler, flowers. The bell-heather and the ling are the common heaths of the plateaux. The cross-leaved heath is more sparsely distributed here because it prefers a moister soil and is, therefore, to be found only on boggy patches. Here and there, twined through the heather (and sometimes also the gorse), you will find the white flowers of dodder, a parasitic plant. Identifying grasses is often none too easy, and is really a job for the specialist, but it should be pointed out that the arid soil of the Forest plateaux forms a stronghold of the bristle-leaved bent grass (*Agrostis setacea*), which is restricted to the southern and southwestern counties of England and to a few places in south Wales, and which is distinctly rare elsewhere in Hampshire. The delightful little hawkbit (*Leontodon autumnalis*), its yellow flowers carried on long stems, is common along the roadside verges from July to October. The ardent botanist will, of course, find much more: but this is not the place for a catalogue.

Nor can there be any need to produce a catalogue of the plants of the broad-leaved woodland. It can scarcely be necessary to say that, where the shade is not too dense, you will find bluebells, wood anemones, wood sorrel, primroses, dog's mercury and ramsons (the wild garlic). But it may be necessary—in order to save the time of the visitor who is in no sense a specialist—to point out that the woodland flora is almost wholly dependent upon the amount of sunlight available. Shade-loving plants do not love deep shade.

This is clearly shown where the ground has been cleared by a fire or where trees have been felled for reafforestation. While the ground is clear, while the newly-planted trees are still small, plenty of light reaches the soil and all kinds of plants flourish: birch, brambles, ragwort, thistles, the wild rose, foxgloves, rose-bay willow-herb, docks and so on.

To digress for a moment. The rosebay willow-herb is something of an enigma. In the older books on British botany you will invariably find it described as widespread but not common. This was certainly an accurate description so far as the Forest was concerned until about mid-way between the wars. It would not be an accurate description today. Those of us old enough will remember the beauty that the rosebay willow-herb brought to the bombed sites of our cities during the war. And since the war it has become very common indeed on waste-land, and in the Forest very common in woodland clearings caused by tree-fellings or fires. The very numerous seeds are, of course, carried long distances by the winds. But there is nothing new in this: it has always been so. And there is nothing new about fellings in woodland, nothing new about woodland fires: these things have always been with us. Why then should the rosebay willow-herb suddenly have taken such a firm hold? Why should it suddenly have increased so greatly? There is here some whim of nature that has not, so far as I am aware, been satisfactorily explained.

To return. On cleared ground there soon springs up a profuse and varied vegetation. But as the trees grow they cast more and more shade, and the number of plants becomes less and less, until in the fully grown conifer plantations there is virtually no undergrowth at all. And you will find that this is so, too, in matured beech woods.

It is the mixed woodland—the woods of oak and beech, holly and yew, birch and chestnut and sycamore, blackthorn and hawthorn—that supports the greatest number and the greatest variety of flowers. Even so, it is on the fringe of the wood and in the rides and glades within the wood, rather than in the heart of the wood, that you are most likely to find flowering plants. There is more light: the shade is less dense.

Again, this is not the place to produce a complete list of the flowers of the woods and their fringes, even if I were capable of doing so. But there are some which must be mentioned. The columbine (*Aquilegia vulgaris*), which is really a plant of limestone, occurs in a few widely separated localities in the Forest. And the Forest can also boast the rich blue lungwort (*Pulmonaria longifolia*), which grows only here and in Dorset and the Isle of Wight: and the rare, oddly-named, bastard palm (*Melittis melissophylum*) with its large white flowers tinged with pink or purple. Both parts of the scientific name, by the way, refer to bees and, though I do not know that bees are particularly addicted to the plant and think that they are not, it would be kinder to call it the honey balm; but then, I suppose, no one would know what was meant. The great rarity of the Forest has still to be mentioned. This is the wild gladiolus (*Gladiolus illyricus*), which is found nowhere else on the mainland of Britain, but which does—or did—occur in the Isle of Wight. I say "or did" because I am not sure that it still does: it may now be extinct. I am sure that in the Forest it is now on the verge of extinction—but, I think, not everywhere quite extinct, though I believe that it is in what was once its favourite locality—partly because ardent gardeners are apt to arrive armed with trowels and dig up the corms in the hope of naturalizing them in their gardens (a hope doomed to disappointment) and partly because picnic parties, not noticing it, trample upon it. I sometimes wish that our wild flowers had a forceful protection society like that which has done so much for our wild birds.

A word must be said about the woodland rides. If you walk these tracks you will soon be surprised to find how boggy they are; so boggy, indeed, that you will find growing in them a number of plants normally associated with true bog and not with the heart of a wood. For example, you will find in most of the ruts formed by the Forestry Commission's vehicles the bulbous rush (*Juncus bulbosus*), which is normally an inhabitant of true bogs. You will also, of course, find the jointed rush (*Juncus articulatus*), but this is normally an inhabitant of wet places—and some of the Forest rides are very wet indeed!

The moist soils of the mixed woodlands give rise to a host of ferns. And now I must restrain myself, for I am a passionate devotee of the whole fern family with the exception of the bracken, a highly successful fern, which is widespread throughout the Forest, on heathland and in woodland alike, and which here, as elsewhere, can be a real nuisance. The graceful lady fern (*Athyrium filixfoemina*) is also very common, especially by stream-sides in light shade. The male fern, the broad shield-fern, the hard fern and the common polypody are also very common. Much rarer is the narrow shield-fern (*Dryopteris lanceolatocristata*) and rare the beech fern (*Thelypteris phegopteris*), which I suppose I ought to describe as very rare, since it is confined to alder swamps and is known to occur in only one locality in the Forest. This is rather surprising for there is plenty of alder in the Forest and it is widespread elsewhere. One fern, which I knew in the Forest in my youth the magnificent Royal fern (*Osmunda regalis*), which grows to a height of six feet or more, has now, so I believe, altogether disappeared. And elsewhere in Britain it can now only be described as occasional. In part, of course, this is due to the draining of the bogs—the march of progress takes little account of the treasures of Nature—but this certainly cannot wholly account for its disappearance from the Forest. Here, again, I fear that the ardent gardener with his trowel must bear some part of the blame.

The Forest can boast many orchids—as many, I suppose, as any other part of England and more than most—some uncommon, some rare, some surprisingly common. The most common, and the most widespread throughout the Forest, is the common twayblade (*Listera ovata*). This is what one would expect, of course, since the plant is found throughout the British Isles with the exception of the Shetland Islands and is the only one of our fifty or so species of orchids to have so wide a distribution. It is a most successful plant because it is able to accommodate itself to a wide variety of habitats, ranging from woodland and comparatively dense shade through grass and heather to bog. But part of its success is, I think, due to the fact that, with its small green flowers, it is one of the least attractive of orchids and certainly one of the least conspicuous. Two other very common Forest orchids are the early purple (*Orchis muscula*) which occurs not only on the heaths, on the fringes of woods and in some of the rides, but also, rather surprisingly, on the roadside verges, and the green-veined or green-winged (*Orchis morio*) which occurs in similar situations, though not, I think, on roadside verges. The latter sometimes occurs in such large numbers that the ground appears purple, so numerous and closely packed are the spikes.

On the open heathland, especially in the southern part of the Forest, are to be found the heath spotted orchid (*Orchis ericetorum*) and the common spotted orchid (*Orchis fuchsii*). For the non-expert it really is not at all easy to tell the two apart unless you have them in the hand for comparison, but in general it would be true to say that the heath spotted orchid has a paler flower than the common spotted orchid and that there are usually fewer flowers on the spike. The spotting is also paler and less definite. But in the Forest, though you may find both growing on open heathland, the heath spotted orchid prefers the drier situations.

Another Forest orchid very tolerant of habitat is the lesser butterfly (*Platanthera bifolia*), which may be found on dry heather-covered slopes and in wet bogs. It is also tolerant of shade and may be found in some of the more open woodlands. The greater butterfly orchid (*Platanthera chlorantha*) also occurs in the Forest, but is much less tolerant of habitat. I have, myself, never found it on heathland nor in boggy conditions, but I have found it in oak-woods and once in fair numbers in a recently felled wood, which suggests that it must be able to survive without flowering for quite

New Forest **beeches**

a long time in fairly dense shade. Both the butterfly orchids are sweetly scented.

Another sweet orchid is the fragrant orchid (*Gymnadenia conopsea*), which, with its dense spikes of pink or lilac flowers, is one of the most attractive of our native orchids. The fragrant orchid is uncommon, which is rather surprising since it is another species remarkably tolerant of habitat, but it does occur in a few localities, most usually on heathland and in association with the heath spotted orchid. But you can never be sure of the fragrant orchid. I have found it in some numbers one year and the next none at all.

This also applies to autumn ladies' tresses (*Spiranthea spiralis*), one of the smallest of our orchids, which may be found in flower as late as mid-October. This is primarily a plant of short turf and in the Forest may be found along the roadside verges and on the lawns, perhaps in the same place for several years in succession and then not at all, and then again, after a lapse of some years, in the same place.

The broad helleborine (*Epipactis helleborine*) might, I suppose, truthfully be described as "plentiful", or at least as "not uncommon", along the fringes of woods and in the rides and glades, since it may be found in such situations often enough. Even so, this is a plant that has to be searched for. It has not the gregarious habit of some of our orchids: finding one does not mean that you are going to find several more in the immediate vicinity. Indeed, I have rarely found more than two at all close together. And so, though I have often come across it, I always have a sense of surprise when I do.

And now, two tragedies—and perhaps a spur to your ambition. Both the marsh helleborine (*Epipactis palustris*), which used to occur in one locality, and the summer ladies' tresses (*Spiranthes aestivalis*), which occurred in two limited localities, now seem to be extinct in the Forest. Indeed, the summer ladies' tresses, which occurred nowhere else in Britain, would now seem to be wholly extinct in Britain. You will notice that I qualify the statement. I use the word "seem" deliberately. As will have been realized, orchids are extremely capricious plants, appearing in one place,

11

Shallow Bog Land

perhaps for years in succession, then disappearing for no apparent reason, and then, perhaps after a lapse of years, suddenly re-appearing again. It is true that the summer ladies' tresses gradually diminished in numbers over a period of years and that it has not been seen for a good many years now. Why this should have happened nobody knows, but it is so long now since it has been seen that it is generally accepted as extinct in Britain. Nevertheless, having regard to the very individual habits of orchids, it is still worth while keeping an eye open. The case of the marsh helle-borine is somewhat different. Its disappearance can probably be attributed to the laying of a pipeline across the marsh where it grew. But this does not mean to say that it will not one day re-establish itself in some other marshy district of the Forest. In his *Wild Orchids of Britain* V. S. Summerhayes records the marsh helleborine from close to the top of the chalk downs near Calne in Wiltshire (a quite exceptional habitat for a damp-loving plant) and says: "The marsh helleborine is known to be very persistent once it becomes established." Again, I think it well worth while keeping an eye open. Though I must admit to having little hope for summer ladies' tresses, it would not surprise me to find the marsh helleborine re-establishing itself.

There remains the real "wet" of the Forest: the true bogs (as opposed to wet heathland or marshland, the ponds and the streams.) For the lover of wildflowers these habitats support treasures in plenty. All the usual plants that thrive in boggy ground and by stream-sides are present, of course: bog asphodel (*Narthecium ossifragium*), marsh valerian (*Valeriana dioica*) and great valerian or all-heal (*Valeriana officinalis*), yellow loosestrife (*Lysimacha vulgaris*) which is a member of the primrose family, and purple loosestrife (*Lythrum salicaria*) which is not, yellow flag (*Iris pseudacorus*), marsh St John's-wort (*Hypericum elodes*) which to the non-expert eye does not look like a St John's-wort at all, common fleabane (*Inula dysenterica*), bulrush or great reed-mace (*Typha latifolia*), both the bur-marigolds (*Bidens cernua* and *Bidens tripartita*), the beautiful marsh wound-wort (*Stachys palustris*), and so on. And in the water, as one would expect, are the water-lilies: the white water-lily (*Nymphea alba*) in comparatively deep, open, still water and the yellow water-lily (*Nuphar lutea*) in running water.

But there are many plants which are not so common and some which are rare: so many, indeed, that I can mention only a few. Near the edges of the bogs you may be fortunate enough to find the beautiful marsh gentian (*Gentiana pneumonanthe*), its flowers sky-blue in autumn. If you are very observant you will see, in July and August, in the shallow sphagnum bogs the tiny pale yellow or yellowish-green flowers of the smallest of all the British orchids, the bog orchid (*Hammarbya paludosa*). It is not all that uncommon—you may, indeed, sometimes find it in quite large numbers—but it is astonishingly easy to overlook. The marsh orchid (*Orchis praetermissa*) is also not uncommon. This is one of the most magnificent of British orchids, the many-flowered spikes being sometimes as much as six inches in length. The flowering season lasts from the beginning of June until at least the middle of July and there is a great variation in the colours of the flowers. The most common colour is a pale purple, but lilac-pink and pale pink are not uncommon, and every now and again pure white specimens may be found. When this does occur, they seem always to be in little groups: it is very rare to find a single white-flowered specimen among plants of other colours.

Seven species of carnivorous plants are to be found in the Forest: three sundews, two bladderworts and two butterworts. The round-leaved sundew (*Drosera rotundifolia*) and the long-leaved sundew (*Drosera intermedia*) are both common, but the great sundew (*Drosera anglica*) is much less plentiful and, perhaps, ought to be described as rare. The flowers of the sundews are white. The common or greater bladderwort (*Utricularia vulgaris*), which has rich yellow flowers borne singly on stalks well above the water, is not uncommon in ditches and pools, especially where the water is brackish. The lesser bladderwort (*Utricularia minor*), the flowers a much paler yellow and projecting only just above the water, is also not uncommon in the pools, but is not, I think, a plant of ditches. The common butterwort (*Pinguicula vulgaris*), the flowers of which are a bright purple, is not as common in the Forest as its name would suggest; no more common, I think, than

the western butterwort (*Pinguicula lusitanica*), its flowers a pale
lilac, which is confined to Ireland, south-western England and
western Scotland and which, I believe, does not occur east of
Southampton Water. All seven plants are eaters of insects, but
their methods of capturing them are very different.

In the sundews the leaves supply the trapping mechanism. The
leaves are green with a number of red patches on them—presumably, the combination or contrast of colours provides an attraction
for insects—and have their margins and upper surfaces covered
with long, hair-like, tentacles. There are about two hundred of
these tentacles to each leaf and each tentacle ends in a club-shaped
swelling covered with a sticky substance which looks like dew:
hence the name. An insect, alighting on a leaf, is caught by this
sticky substance. Immediately this happens the tentacles bend
over towards the mid-rib of the leaf, so that the insect is pressed
firmly against the surface of the leaf. The trap has closed: there is
now no possibility of escape. The club-shaped swellings then
secrete digestive juices, which dissolve the nitrogen-containing
parts of the insect so that they may be absorbed by the plant. As
soon as this has happened the tentacles move back to their
original position, the leaf opens out once more, and the remains
of the insect are either blown away by the wind or washed
away. If you come across a sundew, you can stimulate the
whole process by gently touching the tentacles with a twig or a
pencil.

The butterworts also use their leaves to trap insects, but the
mechanism is different. The oval leaves have their upper surfaces
covered with a pale yellow sticky substance which looks rather
like butter: hence the name. Again, the colour is, presumably,
attractive to insects. When the insect alights on a leaf it is trapped
by this sticky substance and cannot escape. (I think that man
developed the fly-paper from observation of the butterwort: at
any rate, the fly-papers of my childhood were always, I remember,
bright yellow.) When the insect has been caught the margins of
the leaf roll over and enclose it, and then tiny little glands in the
upper surface of the leaf secrete the digestive juices which dissolve
the nitrogen-containing parts of the insect. The meal absorbed,

the leaf opens out again. As with the sundew, the whole process can be stimulated by using a pencil or a twig.

Unlike the sundews and the butterworts, which are terrestrial plants, the bladderworts are completely submerged aquatics, whose finely divided leaves, borne on long stems, float on or just beneath the surface of the water. Some of the leaf segments become modified into bladder-like structures, from which the plant gets its name and which are the mechanism by which small aquatic creatures are captured. Each bladder has one opening, inside which there is a valve which can only open inwards. An animal, entering the opening, is in a sort of ante-chamber and is quite safe, since the valve is closed and the bladder not distended. But within the ante-chamber there are a number of tiny hairs and when the animal touches these the valve opens, water is drawn into the bladder, which becomes distended, and the animal is sucked in with the water. The inner surface wall of the bladder is furnished with glands, which secrete the digestive juices. The whole process from the moment of capture to the end of absorption and the return of the bladder to normal takes, as a rule, about twenty minutes. The bladder, by the way, is capable of very considerable expansion: it has been calculated at as much as 88 per cent. The whole arrangement is most ingenious. And it should be remembered that the bladderwort is a plant which definitely captures its prey: the animal does not force its way past the valve, the plant opens its valve and captures its prey.

The seeker after the wild flowers of the Forest must be prepared to walk. And the walker in the Forest will need three things: stout footwear, a good map, and a compass. The Forest is really quite remarkably wet; much, much wetter than anyone, accustomed to traversing it on main roads in a car, would imagine possible. There are streams everywhere and except for a few weeks in the driest of seasons (and they occur very infrequently in England; about once in ten years, as a matter of fact) it is all too common to come across patches of deep mud, patches of ground not far removed from swamp, in the most unexpected places. Moreover, the woodland rides are often clothed with tall, rank, and very wet grasses. Stout footwear is absolutely essential.

Essential, too, are a good map and a compass. Now, this may sound silly, when one considers the size of the Forest, when one remembers that it is quite impossible, at any point in the Forest, to be more than a couple of miles from a road. Let me repeat that a good map and a compass are essential. One may be no more than a couple of miles from a road, nevertheless it is all too easy to get lost. True, one is unlikely to be lost for very long; but one can easily get lost for long enough to ruin the whole day's expedition. I speak from experience. I think that I may claim to know the Forest pretty well, yet, walking without map or compass, confident that I knew just where I was going, I have been lost more than once. Indeed, on one occasion my sister and I (and we were not then children) managed to get lost in one of the enclosures within a couple of miles of our home! Undoubtedly, the best map is the Ordnance Survey 1:25,000 (two and a half inch) scale. With this and a compass one should be able to follow paths and tracks through the Forest without difficulty. With the map alone you will not find it so simple.

Now, it is possible to walk right across the Forest at its greatest width, from north-west to south-east, in a day. I have done so. But this gives a quite misleading impression of the whole. Within the borders of the Forest there are many miles—I do not know how many; many hundreds certainly—of paths and tracks open to the walker, and it is these—the paths and tracks through the inclosures and over the heaths—that will be of interest to the botanically-minded. It is from these that one can walk, sometimes only a few yards, over open country to find some treasure. Sometimes it is on these that one can find that treasure.

In a book such as this it is obviously impossible even to outline all the many walks, short and of a fair distance, available to the seeker after flowers or birds or insects. And I know of no modern book devoted solely to walking the Forest. Joan Begbie's *Walking in the New Forest*, which was published in 1934, has long been out of print. But it is not too difficult to obtain second-hand copies and it is still valuable for the purpose. Thirty odd years have seen many changes in the Forest, but surprisingly few that seriously affect the walker in its inmost recesses. But let me give you one or two of my favourite walks: none of them very long.

Starting from Brockenhurst, take the main Lyndhurst road to the bridge at Balmer Lawn and then follow the winding stream as it runs beneath the side of Black Knowl Heath and skirts New Park Enclosure. The path leads through Queen's Bower and Queen's Bower is enchanting with its little streams—three join here—and its little bridge and huge shady oaks and, in the season of the year, bracken that is waist high. I do not know why it is called Queen's Bower, and I have not met anyone who does know nor anyone who has been able to put forward any but the obvious explanation: that some queen liked the place very much and used to come here with the maidens of her court. But, if that is correct, why no record of her coming? The movements of royalty rarely pass unrecorded. If any queen held her court here, then I think that it would have been some nameless, but beautiful, siren of Brockenhurst. This is a great place for moths and butterflies, and is said to be one of the haunts of that monarch of the woodlands, the Purple Emperor. But, though I have taken the Purple Emperor elsewhere in the Forest, I have not myself seen one here.

The stream runs on between little sandy banks, clear and shallow and amber above a gravel bed, so clear that one may watch the shoals of tiny fish darting here and there at incredible speed. Here there are oaks on either hand, their roots drinking of the stream, their branches meeting and inter-lacing overhead, and reflected as a maze in the water beneath. A little further on beeches replace the oaks and the stream, still perfectly clear, runs deeper, eating away the sand from the roots so that they stand exposed as great knotted sinews. In some places the banks are crowned with bracken and in others with smooth mossy turf, and in these latter places you may see the signs where the deer have come down to drink. A little further on there is a ford where the stream runs over a smooth gravel bed, and rounding a bend widens into quite a broad and quite a deep pool. A good place, this, for the botanically-minded and a good place also for dragonflies. I remember this as a dragonfly place particularly well, because I had here my first lesson in the duplicity of man. It was here, as a boy, that I caught a

dragonfly of a kind that I have never seen since, and whose name
I have never known. But I remember that dragonfly very well
indeed. It was small, perhaps only an inch or so long, and it was a
beautiful emerald green with an orange moustache and orange
spots on its wings. I was very pleased with it and took it home
and showed it to my schoolmaster, a keen entomologist, who was
then staying with us and collecting moths and butterflies in the
Forest. He was also very pleased with it, and I did not see it again.

A little beyond this pool the path reaches the Lyndhurst–
Bournemouth road. And here you have the choice of two walks.
You can follow the stream, which is named Highland Water, up
to Highland Water Inclosure and then through to Puckpits and
over Withybed Bottom to the Ringwood–Cadnam road (and
that is a very lovely walk) or you can turn left down the main
road, which here runs for a short distance through open country
with heather and gorse and scattered hawthorns. This is the easier
walking of the two, and leads to some of the most famous features
of the Forest.

Where the trees come down to the road again, there are two
gates. That on the left leads into Vinney Ridge Inclosure, which
I have always regarded as a favourite haunt of grey squirrels, but
which is otherwise rather dull. That on the right leads into Knightwood Inclosure. This, which is now tarred and suitable for
motors, is the one to take. Knightwood is an enclosure of giant
conifers, arrayed in orderly ranks, but in the midst of a grove of
beech, some of them giants in themselves, stands the Knightwood
Oak, dwarfing them all, a tree of immense girth. If you really
want to appreciate the Knightwood Oak properly, then you
should see the Eagle Oak, half-a-mile away on your left hand,
which also has the distinction (along with the Peter Oak) of being
marked on the Ordnance Survey map. If you see the Eagle Oak
first, you will be unlikely to believe that there could be a bigger
oak anywhere. You come to the Knightwood Oak and you
marvel that you should have been so impressed with the Eagle
Oak. I cannot do better than to quote what I have already written
about the Knightwood Oak. "It is supposed to be the oldest and
largest oak in England and as its girth at shoulder-height is

twenty-two feet I think that it is quite likely that it is all that it is claimed to be. . . . This great tree was here, though no more than a seedling, when Stephen was ruling a troubled kingdom. It was here, a mere boy, when John was signing the Magna Charta. It was here, nearing maturity, when Edward I was settling things in Wales. It was here, a sturdy man, when the Armada sailed to destruction. It watched its neighbours and its friends being cut down to make the ships to fight Napoleon. It watched its friends fall before the fury of the storm and the cold precision of the axe. It heard the news of Waterloo and Inkerman, and Lucknow and Mafeking, and Ypres and Verdun. In its old age it heard of Dunkirk and Tobruk, of Caen and Falaise, of Stalingrad and Cassino. In its old age it heard the whistle of bombs (a very large number fell in the New Forest) and the drone of the bombers on their way to Coventry, and later the same drone on the way to Hamburg and Cologne. It has seen kings come and go and dictators rise and fall. It has watched, year upon year, men make love in just the same way and in much the same words. It has watched, year upon year, all those things that we, each generation of us, consider new and exciting, new and terrifying. And each year in October its leaves come spinning to the ground. They have done so now maybe eight hundred times. I have a feeling that it will be shedding its leaves long after I have joined the many thousands of Forest men that have died since it was born."

This is a short walk, a matter of three or four miles, but if you have taken it as all Forest walks should be taken, slowly, stopping to stand and stare and listen, stopping to appreciate the beauty of this plant and that, it will have taken you quite a long time. You can, of course, go on through Mark Ash Wood (now a Nature Reserve) and Bolderwood Grounds and up the Bratley Water to the Ringwood–Cadnam road. And this is only a further couple of miles or so, and not difficult walking. But, if you are new to the Forest, then I would advise you to turn back at the Knightwood Oak, cross the Lyndhurst–Bournemouth road, and enter Vinney Ridge Inclosure at the gate immediately opposite. The ride here has also been tarred and is suitable for motor-cars. But it is really very much better to walk it, because it leads to the Ornamental

Drive. The Ornamental Drive is something quite apart from the Forest of the enclosures and open woodlands and heaths: more in the nature of an arboretum. It is a feature of the Forest which every visitor should make a point of seeing. Here there are giant sequoias, their boles glowing, and many other specimen trees, and many of them are labelled. (Trees are also labelled in Bolderwood Grounds, by the way.) It is more than worth while spending some time in the Ornamental Drive, studying these trees; which is why you should walk, for continually stopping the car makes of the whole affair a nuisance. Many of the trees in the Ornamental Drive occur elsewhere in the Forest and it gives one a fine sense of achievement to be able to identify them correctly, which is just what the Ornamental Drive enables you to do. From the Ornamental Drive you can walk across Ober Heath, part of which has recently been taken into a new enclosure, and then you are back on the western edge of Black Knowl: back pretty well where you started.

Another favourite walk of mine is down Bratley Water and through Oakley Inclosure to Burley. There is about a mile of open heathland, much frequented by stonechats, between the Ringwood–Cadnam road and Oakley Inclosure and then you drop downhill and into the woodland. Oakley is the largest enclosure in the Forest and is intersected by innumerable paths and rides. Taking a glance at the Ordnance Survey One-inch map, it would seem to be the easiest thing in the world to walk straight through it, keeping pretty well due south. But this is a very big wood and it is all too easy to take the wrong path at an intersection, the wrong ride at a fork. I am fully aware that, if you look at a large-scale map, this sounds unbelievable: but Oakley is the easiest place in the world in which to get lost, even if you know the Forest well. And I say that, having known Oakley for the better part of my life. This is the wood in which my sister and I, then in our late teens, once got lost: and we should have known where we were, for we lived in Burley, virtually on the edge of it. We spent a long time walking down tracks that got narrower and narrower and finally lost themselves in the undergrowth: we stumbled in and out of bogs, and crossed tiny meandering streams, with no real idea of the direction in which we were travelling (the sun is not of much use in Oakley even in high summer and this was an October afternoon); the light began to fade (and the light dies very quickly in deep woodland in autumn) and it was thick dusk, when suddenly—and when we least expected it—we came on to a track we both recognized. We certainly were not frightened, but I think that we were both a little uneasy. I know that I was, for I felt then—and I have had the same feeling once or twice since, as the light has died in autumn and winter and I have been in deep woodland—the hostility of the Forest. I know that I was very glad to see that track and to know just where I was; even though it was humiliating to realize how far off-course I was. So, if you take this walk, take the large-scale map with you; and take a compass too. It is a very beautiful walk and, from the moment you enter Oakley to the moment you leave it, you will be very unlikely to meet a soul.

With Burley as starting point there are a number of excellent walks of varying lengths. Two to Brockenhurst can be particularly recommended, for they show such very different aspects of the Forest. The first is to pick up Ober Water on Burley Lawn and to follow it—you will not need either map or compass, but this is not quite so easy as it sounds because the ground is pretty difficult in places—by Red Rise and over the Bournemouth road, past Aldregehill Inclosure to its junction with Highland Water, and so down to Balmer Lawn and Brockenhurst. For almost the whole of this walk you have on your left hand, on the far bank of the stream, deep woodland and on your right hand, heath, bog, marsh, and (every now and again) lawn. There is no clear path or track along the stream and the ground is often very wet indeed, so you will need stout footgear. At first sight Ober Water may seem a dullish stream—it is certainly not a beautiful one by comparison with many of the Forest streams—but it does form a boundary, so to speak, between two of the main types of Forest land and it is much used by the wild life of the Forest. It holds fish (and bigger fish than its size would lead one to suppose) and, though I cannot remember ever seeing a man fishing it, I have seen kingfishers more than once and I think that there has been a heron somewhere along it every time I have walked its length. Both the ponies and the cattle drink from it, of course, and so do the deer of a morning before we are up to see them. And a great many birds use it, particularly at migration times, perhaps because so few humans do. In fact, this can be one of the most interesting and exciting (and foot-wetting!) walks in the Forest.

The other walk to Brockenhurst is by way of Burley Beacon. Take the road over the railway track and about two hundred yards after you have crossed it turn left on to Holmesley Ridge. There are no well-defined paths here, though plenty of pony paths; and you should take one of these. It may not be the right one—almost certainly it will not be—but it will join up with others to lead you to a small pond, to which a surprising number of birds come at all seasons of the year and in which, in summer, there are usually some magnificent crested newts. If you go on walking eastwards along the ridge—be careful to keep to the pony paths, for there are quite a lot of unsuspected boggy places dotted about and the ponies know the best ground and keep to it—you will come to Holmesley Lodge, and here you should take the track that leads back over the railway and on to Goatpen Plain. Goatpen has some surprisingly steep little hills and in the hollows some fascinating boggy patches, some of which support most interesting plants. On the far side of Goatpen you must cross the Bournemouth road at Wilverley Post—at week-ends a very hazardous crossing indeed—and then you have three miles or so of moorland, dipping and rising and dipping again, and in places very boggy indeed, to Brockenhurst. This is pretty wild country.

But the wildest, least frequented, area of the Forest lies to the north-west of the Ringwood–Cadnam road. I think that this area is best explored in, so to speak, short bursts: by leaving the car somewhere off the road (there are a number of places where this can be done) or by taking the bus either from Ringwood or Cadnam, leaving it where the fancy takes you, and then walking for just as far as you wish before returning to the main road. The northern part of the area can be explored in the same way from the Cadnam–Downton and Cadnam–Fordingbridge roads. Walking from a fixed centre—and there are really only five, all on the periphery of the area: Bramshaw, Cadnam, Fordingbridge, Ringwood and Stoney Cross—imposes great restriction on the explorer and also involves much longer distances than most holiday-makers will be willing to undertake. But, with the aid of a large-scale map and a compass, it is possible to plan some very beguiling walks out-and-back from a car or a bus.

If you stand at Picket Post and look north-eastwards along the line of the Ringwood–Cadnam road, you are looking along the line of another of the Forest's natural boundaries, along the line of a major watershed. To your right all the streams run south-eastwards to the Solent and Southampton Water: to your left all the streams run south-westwards to the Avon and so to Christchurch Harbour. These streams run through a series of almost parallel, well-defined, valleys, separated by gravel ridges or plateaux, which rise gradually to reach the highest point within the Forest perambulation near Telegraph Post. This is, in fact, only 419 feet above sea-level, but it seems and feels much higher and the views of the chalklands to the north and west are superb. There ought, of course, also to be superb views to the south, but Islands Thorns Inclosure shuts off the distance. There is, however, an eye-stretching expanse of moorland.

If you want to see deer in daylight, you stand a better chance of doing so in this part of the Forest than anywhere else. There are often fallow deer to be seen at the eastern end of Great Linford Inclosure and in the valley formed by the Linford Brook— judging by the names here, Roe Wood Inclosure and Red Shoot Wood, this has always been a favourite haunt of deer—and I have also seen fair numbers of fallow deer along the valley of Dockens Water and on the confines of Amberwood Inclosure. There are roe deer to be seen too, if you are lucky. I have seen them near Islands Thorns Inclosure and in Long Bottom near Pitts Wood. Seeing deer in daylight in the Forest (though you may sometimes see some in Rhinefield) is unusual and always a matter of chance. But the deer in this part of the Forest, though naturally wary, do not seem to be unduly perturbed by the presence of man; provided that one behaves with due circumspection, it is even possible to approach fairly close. I suppose that this is due to the fact that there are few motorable roads and those few narrow and tortuous, and, therefore, few people about. The whole area is wild and lonely: in pleasant contrast to what is happening elsewhere in the Forest.

VIII

THE NEW FOREST: FUTURE

THE official boundaries of the New Forest today enclose an area of about 144 square miles. Of this area about forty-two square miles —almost all of which lies in Beaulieu, Brockenhurst, Burley, Lyndhurst and their immediate surroundings—are in private ownership. All the rest is in public ownership, most of it Crown land (as it is called), and is, with a few minor exceptions, open to the public for their enjoyment.

The area is administered by the Forestry Commission. The chief concern of the Forestry Commission—though it must pay some attention to safeguarding public amenities and the protection of wild life—is timber production. And this means, of course, that everyone living within the Forest boundaries—and, though to less extent, everyone visiting the Forest—and all wild life (fauna and flora) within the Forest boundaries is affected by the activities of the Forestry Commission.

It would be idle to pretend that this is an easy area to administer. As will have been realized from the chapter on the "Background", it never has been. It is precisely because it has been so difficult to administer that it maintained, until quite recently, its character. In fact, its character was maintained by the character of its people, the "Commoners" who, perhaps from Norman times, fought strenuously for their "rights". It will be advisable, in view of the present situation, to outline the salient points in this long fight again.

I do not think that anybody knows just how these "common rights" originated, but the Commoners' insistence upon them was such that they were finally given statutory recognition by the

Act of 1698: recognition which was renewed by the Act of 1808. Neither Act satisfied the Commoners and the continued trouble over rights led to the New Forest Act of 1851 (the Deer Removal Act), which not only provided for the removal of the deer, but gave to the Crown, as compensation for the loss of deer, the right to enclose a further 10,000 acres for the growth of timber. But the Act went much further than that. It also gave to the Crown "rolling powers"; that is, the power to remove fences when the timber had grown sufficiently to be safe from attack by the Commoners' animals and to re-erect them to enclose a further area. Obviously, if this policy had been enforced, there would in due course have been no common-land at all: and the deer, though their numbers had been drastically reduced, had not been removed.

It was solely because the Commoners fought the 1851 Act so energetically that the Act of 1877 (known as the "Commoners' Charter") came into force. This Act abolished the "rolling powers" of the Crown, allowed the Commoners to turn their animals into the Forest throughout the year in return for a small annual payment, and reconstituted the Court of Verderers. On paper at least, it changed the whole relationship between the Crown and the Commoners. Unfortunately, it was not a good piece of Parliamentary draughtsmanship. It left any number of loopholes for controversy and consequent bickering, and it did not provide the Verderers (whose qualifications were so defined that they were most unlikely to oppose officialdom) with adequate finance. Friction between the Crown and the Commoners continued almost without pause and with increasing irritation on both sides until the New Forest Act of 1949.

The 1877 Act defined the qualifications for an elective Verderer as the *ownership* of not less than seventy-five acres to which were attached Right of Common of Pasture: and the election was not by secret ballot. (It is not altogether surprising that there were only two elections between 1877 and 1947!) The 1949 Act made the ballot secret and defined the qualification of an elector (who must be over twenty-one) as the *occupation* of not less than one acre carrying with it Right of Common of Pasture. The Verderers'

Silver Birches: the native trees of the Forest

Court—next to the Coroner's Court the oldest judiciary court in England—as now constituted consists of an Official Verderer appointed by the Crown, five elected Verderers and four appointed Verderers; one by the Minister of Agriculture, one by the Forestry Commission, one by the Hampshire County Planning Committee, and one by a body specifically concerned with amenity. The Verderers appointed by the Minister of Agriculture and by the Forestry Commission are not allowed to vote on matters in which they have a special interest. All very fair and above-board.

The 1877 Act made the drainage of the open Forest the responsibility of the Verderers; a responsibility which they could not possibly fulfil, since they were denied the necessary funds. The 1949 Act has made it the legal responsibility of the Forestry Commission to ensure that the whole of the Forest is properly drained and the grazing properly maintained, thus relieving the Verderers of a heavy financial burden. And by giving to the Verderers power to make and alter by-laws (after consultation with the Minister of Agriculture), allowing them in this way to raise marking-fees, and by allowing the Forestry Commission, subject to permission from the Verderers and upon payment to them, to enclose up to 5,000 acres for the growing of timber, the 1949 Act gave them financial independence.

The Verderers now employ four Agisters—before the 1949 Act they could afford to employ only two—to see that their by-laws are obeyed and to collect marking-fees. (Agisters, by the way, must not be confused with Keepers, who are employees of the Forestry Commission.) Each Agister has his own district and each district its own particular method of marking. The Commoners' animals run in the Forest by Right of Common Pasture, but this is only one of a number of common rights. These are:

Right of Common Pasture of Sheep. There can be no doubt that there are still a few holdings to which this right is attached. It was never widely used and it has not been used for many years past.

Right of Common of Marl. There are said to be about a score of

12

Self-sown conifers in the Forest

marl-pits in the Forest. I should doubt if one has been used in recent years, because there are now so many less energetic ways of manuring the land.

Right of Common of Turbary. At one time, when turves were widely used for fuel, this was an important and most valuable right. There are cottages in the Forest with fireplaces specially built for burning peat, and turves are still cut occasionally. But, with the introduction of modern fuels and the paraffin-oil heater especially, the right is inevitably falling into disuse.

Right of Common of Estover. Estover is a Norman word which means, roughly, the collection of fuelwood. The Commoners maintained that they had the right to take as much fuelwood as they could gather "by hook or by crook". The "crook" was a long pole, fashioned like a shepherd's crook, and was used to dislodge dead wood from the branches of the trees: the "hook" was a sharp bill-hook, which was used to cut growing wood not thick enough to require an axe. The hook could do a great deal of damage and its use was, understandably, unpopular with the authorities. Indeed, the whole right was extremely unpopular with the authorities, who did everything in their power to discourage its exercise. The right is still attached to a few holdings, but is no longer exercised. Instead, by agreement, the Forestry Commission provides a few loads of firewood annually to those holdings with Right of Common of Estover.

Right of Common of Mast. This is the right to turn pigs into the Forest during the pannage season (25 September to 22 November), subject to certain by-laws. All pigs must first be inspected by an Agister on the Commoner's holding, must be properly ringed and marked, and a fee of ten shillings per pig must be paid. Until quite recently the right was fairly widely used, but it is now quite uncommon to see a pig loose in the Forest. In addition the Commoners have acquired the right—it is not, however, a "Common Right", a legally recognized right—to turn their breeding-sows into the Forest throughout the year, provided that they are returned to their holdings at night. Again, this right was fairly widely used until quite recently.

Right of Common of Pasture of Commonable Animals. Commonable animals are horses, ponies, cattle and donkeys. (Though geese and chickens are not, strictly speaking, commonable animals, they seem to have been allowed to wander in the Forest from time immemorial without objection.) This is the most widespread and the most widely used of all the Common Rights. But the Commoner has to observe a number of by-laws covering inspection of stallions, disease, viciousness, and so on. Furthermore, commonable animals can only be turned on to the Forest after they have been branded with the owner's brand (which must first be approved by the Verderers) and, in the case of ponies, tail-marked by the Agister of the district. The tail-marking fee is fifteen shillings for each animal.

These Common Rights do not belong to a person but to a holding, and pass with the holding to the occupier. The rights vary with each holding, but most (I think all) carry the Right of Common of Pasture.

This does not, of course, mean that every occupier exercises his rights. Until fairly recently every occupier probably did do so. When I was a boy, this was almost certainly the case. In those days men exercised rights—marl, mast, turbary, estover—which have now fallen wholly into disuse. Today, even the most widespread of all the Common Rights—the Right of Common of Pasture— is exercised by comparatively few and these few decrease in numbers year by year. No longer does every Commoner have his cow, his pig, his pony. The old pattern has almost disappeared. The Forest is changing.

The change may be said to have begun in 1926. The "climate" had begun to alter before that, of course. It began to change at the end of the first World War, with the coming of the *nouveau riche*, wholly urban or suburban in outlook. But it was in 1926 that the change in "climate" first became manifest. Up to that time the gypsies had been free to camp wherever they wished on the open Forest, provided that they moved on every forty-eight hours. And, it should be remembered, they had been doing this for nearly four hundred years. In 1926 they were rounded up and herded into compounds. The action was a direct contravention of the 1877 Act. But the gypsies had no organization and there were few to speak on their behalf: too few to carry weight. Into the compounds they went. It is interesting to consider why this action was taken. Why was it considered necessary to interfere with an age-old custom, with a traditional way of life? Nobody seems to know. It is generally believed that there was a spontaneous outcry by the residents in the Forest against the gypsies and their habits; against their litter and their thieving ways. But many books have been written about the gypsies of the New Forest in the days when they were free to wander where they wished and in not one of them have I been able to find any mention of hostility on the part of the residents. I can remember no hostility myself—which is not to say that the gypsies were loved—and I do not recall that they left behind them much litter. Of course, there were losses. Of course holly was taken at Christmas time and daffodils at the time of their flowering: of course the occasional chicken disappeared and it was always the gypsies who were blamed, never the fox. But these things were accepted as among the normal hazards of Forest life. There was certainly no hostility to gypsies as such—no Forest pub would refuse to serve a gypsy—and certainly there was no outcry against them before the first World War. But after that war there was a fresh influx of newly-wealthy townsfolk, people jealous of their status, and with their coming one began to hear complaints about this and that, about thieving and particularly about insanitary conditions in the Forest wherever gypsies had camped. For the first time there was a complete lack of understanding of the gypsy way of life, a complete lack of sympathy with it. Not among the Commoners: the Commoners had lived with gypsies on their doorsteps for generations, knew them and knew how to deal with them, accepted them as part of the Forest way of life. But that men and women, nomads with no visible means of support, should be able to camp freely in the Forest was an affront to those who, newly come to wealth, had paid hard cash for the privilege of doing so. To these people the gypsies somehow let the "tone" of the place down. Money in Britain talks pretty loudly. Into the compounds went the gypsies. And that, unpalatable though it may be, was the basic truth of the matter.

The New Forest Committee 1947, which was appointed "to

investigate the state and condition of the New Forest and, having due regard to existing rights and interests, to recommend such measures as they consider desirable and necessary for adjusting the Forest to modern requirements", had this to say of the gypsies:

> While the standard of living throughout the country is steadily being raised, a group is allowed to live in the Forest which has hardly reached the standard of the Stone Age. The gypsies, it is true, have not been heard in their own defence, but we have visited their camps and we should hesitate to describe them in detail. Even the picturesque element which appeals to the imagination of their defenders is here entirely lacking. Whatever may have been the case in earlier times, those of to-day show little of the true Romany strain and a very few only maintain the old Romany way of life with its comparatively high standards.

It is difficult to believe this: but that appeared in a British Government White Paper. British Government White Papers are usually monuments to the thoroughness and impartiality of those appointed to conduct an investigation. This one, at least so far as the gypsies are concerned, is evidence of a shameful departure from the normal high standard.

Why were no gypsies heard? Could it be that the august members of the Committee could not bring themselves to sit at the same table as the "unwashed"? But, even if that (inexcusable though it would be) were so, surely the Committee could have heard one or two people who were familiar with gypsies, could have heard one or two authorities on the gypsy way of life? They did not do so. Indeed, they made no attempt to do so; none whatsoever. Instead, the Committee—not one of whom had, in all probability, ever seen an earth-closet, let alone used one—visited the compounds and were appalled by the conditions they found: and rightly appalled. The conditions then were dreadful: as, indeed, they still are. "The gypsies, it is true, were not heard in their own defence." You will notice that it is the gypsies who, by implication, are blamed for these conditions by the Committee. There is no mention of the fact that they were herded into these compounds; there is no mention of the fact that the compounds either had no water at all or water in most inadequate supply: there is no mention of the fact that no sanitary arrangements whatsoever were provided. Of course, the conditions were appalling—are appalling—but the blame for this does not rest with the gypsies. It rests squarely on the shoulders of those who, to "protect" this or that interest, forced them into the compounds . . . and then did nothing for them. The Committee did nothing for them either. True, it made some studiously vague suggestions for "reform", but there was never any suggestion that the compounds should be abolished. There was never any suggestion that the gypsies should be allowed to resume their ancient custom of camping where they wished on the open Forest. There was never any realization that the solitary camp of a gypsy family, moved every forty-eight hours, constituted no danger, was more sanitary, was infinitely healthier in every way than the compound. There was no realization that it was the compound system itself that was at fault. But then the gypsies were not represented before the Committee, were not articulate, were not organized. They were, therefore, unimportant.

I draw attention to this passage in the Report of the New Forest Committee because it is symptomatic of an attitude of mind: an attitude of mind which is responsible for much of the change which has already come to the Forest, an attitude of mind which must, inevitably, change the Forest almost out of recognition in the future.

Now, I must make it clear that, except for the passages concerning the gypsies, I have nothing against the Report of the New Forest Committee. In every other way it was a wholly excellent Report. The interests of all the articulate and of all the organized bodies—the Commoners, the other residents, the town visitors, the naturalists, and those concerned with forestry—were considered most carefully and some extremely valuable recommendations were made. Indeed, it may be said that on the whole, and as conditions were at that time, the Report went a long way towards preserving the New Forest for the future. In the light of events since its publication one can see that it would have been a very good thing for the New Forest had the Committee's Report been adopted in full. But, as is the way of Governments, some of the essentials in the Report were disregarded when it came to framing the New Forest Act 1949. In particular, the Act did nothing to bring the whole of the New Forest within one rural district council and it ignored what was a really fundamental recommendation; namely, that the boundaries be greatly extended to bring the adjacent commons within the perambulation. That was a farsighted suggestion: failure to adopt it a great mistake.

But, in the main, the Act did incorporate the recommendations of the Committee. It did establish a new Verderers' Court: it did establish the power of the Verderers to make and alter by-laws: it did establish the responsibility of the Forestry Commission for the drainage of the Forest: it did establish the relative rights of the Forestry Commission, the Commoners, and the general public. And all that was to the good.

But it did something else as well: something which is not, I think, even yet fully understood. It re-established the "rolling powers": or, rather, it has established new "rolling powers", granted not to the Forestry Commission, but to the Ministry of Agriculture. Under the Act the Minister of Agriculture may approach the Verderers for permission to enclose parts of the Forest, up to a limit of 3,000 acres, for cultivation. The enclosed land may be cropped for a period of years—the period is not specified, but must be agreed with the Verderers—and must then be returned as pasture. On its return, the Verderers may control the grazing in any way they consider desirable to preserve the pasture. A clause is inserted to the effect that any such enclosure shall not keep the public off highways. But that, surely, is rather beside the point. The point is that great areas of the Forest could now be enclosed by the Ministry of Agriculture and, on return, retained as enclosures by the Verderers. The fact is that there is now a legal possibility of enclosing 3,000 acres of the Forest and of retaining such enclosures indefinitely either in the hands of the Ministry of Agriculture or of the Verderers: a legal possibility, moreover, of making fresh enclosures as soon as the improved land has been handed back to the Verderers. And one can be quite certain that provision for such enclosures to be made was not inserted into the Act for no reason at all.

Now, it is true that, when the Act was passed, there must have seemed little likelihood of the Commoners ever agreeing to any such measure of enclosure. Apart from the Official Verderer, five of the nine Verderers are elected by the Commoners and the Verderer appointed by the Ministry of Agriculture would not be allowed to vote in a debate on any such measure of enclosure. The Commoners would, therefore, have the majority vote in any such debate. It may be assumed that they would never agree to any such measure. It may also be assumed that, supposing such a measure was agreed, the Verderers (the representatives of the Commoners still holding the majority vote) would impose a limit of, say, five years—that would, indeed, be about the minimum if the land was to be improved—and that they would not, on return, maintain such enclosures for long.

These—though the last is very optimistic: all history goes to show that once land is enclosed, it has an obstinate tendency to remain that way!—may well have been valid assumptions in 1949. Whether they are today is quite another matter. Events have overtaken the Forest. The situation as it was in 1949 does not hold good today in any single particular.

Let us, first, consider the roads. I quote from the Report of the New Forest Committee 1947:

The future development of the Forest roads must be largely dependent on the variation of road traffic to be expected during the next decade. That is an unknown quantity at present but it is reasonable to suppose that the increase will be considerable, at any rate towards the end of the period, as more cars become available. The policy of the County Council as explained to us was as follows: All their plans are directed to coaxing as much as possible of the through traffic to the new Trunk Road. . . . The proposed road from Totton to Christchurch via Hythe and Lymington, named in the Planning Reports the Southern Circular Road, is not regarded as a high priority. In fact unless the strip of land between the Forest and Southampton Water is industrialized, a change which planning is directed to prevent, it should not be needed.

The last sentence was prompted by a paragraph in the South

ampton Planning Report 1945, which dealt with the south-western side of Southampton Water in these words:

> From these observations it would seem that the time is not opportune for development here, and unless something quite unforeseen were to happen, which would justify the expense that must necessarily be involved, most of the area in question should be preserved as "agricultural", it having a great amenity value to Southampton as open country bordering the New Forest.

The "quite unforeseen" has happened. At Fawley there is now the largest oil refinery in Europe and there are the ancillary industries. There is already heavy industrialization in the area, and there will, of course, be more. It would be foolish to suppose otherwise. The Southern Circular Road, not regarded as a high priority in 1947, is now a distinct possibility. Indeed, with the further industrialization of the western shore of Southampton Water (which will surely take place), its construction in the possibly not distant future must be regarded as inevitable.

Which brings me back to the "new Trunk Road", which is, in fact, the old Ringwood–Cadnam road (A31). A portion of this is now dual-carriageway, and it is evident that this dual-carriageway will in due course be extended. The proposal to turn the old main road into a fast modern trunk road received careful attention from the Committee. I quote again:

> We discussed this proposal in great detail with the County Council representative, the Verderers, the Commoners, and the representatives of the Automobile Association and The Royal Automobile Club, and in the course of these discussions received some very valuable suggestions. At the outset both Commoners and road users were unanimous that animals must be kept off the roads. In its extreme form this was expressed in a suggestion that all main roads should be fenced. Consideration of expense, the effect on amenities and engineering difficulties ruled this out as inadvisable. This decided us to treat the Trunk Road as a separate problem and it was proposed that following the precedent of the railway it should be fenced and cattle creeps or tunnels provided at frequent intervals so that the Commoners' animals had access to all parts of the Forest. This was also open to certain objections. One was the serious effect

on the amenities of long lines of fence in what has always been an open space and another was that the fence would have to have gates, and gates are apt to be left open. A group of ponies on the road between the two fences would be more dangerous than if there were no fences at all. We are indebted to Captain Sutton of Brockenhurst for the suggestion of a ha-ha fence . . . The ha-ha has the double advantage of saving the amenities and solving the problem of gates.

Needless to say, there is no ha-ha. The road is fenced on both sides. Captain Sutton's suggestion and the Committee's acceptance of it were admirable, but when it came to the point of decision other interests, other considerations, prevailed and "amenity" was brushed aside.

The road is fenced with two cattle-grids, one on each side; to permit access to the Forest by motorists, to prevent egress from the Forest by the Commoners' animals. No longer are their ponies and cattle on the Ringwood–Cadnam road; and this is a good thing. But the praiseworthy intention of the Committee to preserve the amenity of what had always been an open space and to allow the Commoners' animals access to all parts of the Forest has been defeated. Indeed, the fencing of the Ringwood–Cadnam road has virtually cut off the north-western part of the Forest from the rest.

And that is not all. There are now cattle-grids on all the roads leading into the Forest. Cattle-grids are useless without fences and so the whole Forest has now been fenced in. Except for the stretch of the Ringwood–Cadnam road, this fencing is unobtrusive. Indeed, in many places it is scarcely noticeable and probably is not noticed by the vast majority of visitors. There can be no question but that it had to be done. It has stopped the Commoners' animals straying, as they used to do, far beyond the Forest perambulation. Before the fencing ponies had been known to go as far as the common in Southampton, and you used to find them (and cattle) far up the Romsey road. There can be no question that, in these days of incessant and heavy traffic, such straying had to be stopped. Nevertheless, there can be no question that this fencing has in some measure altered the character of the Forest. Moreover, it—and especially the fencing of the Ringwood–Cadnam road—has set a precedent which must, inevitably, be followed elsewhere in due course.

With the exception of the Ringwood–Cadnam trunk road, the main roads within the Forest boundary are not fenced. The Cadnam–Brockenhurst road (A337) and the Ashurst–Christchurch road (A35), both of which pass through Lyndhurst and both of which carry a great deal of fast-moving traffic, which increases in volume annually, are unfenced. On both these roads, but particularly on A35, accidents involving commonable animals are distressingly frequent and the principal cause of these accidents is speed. A simple solution would be to impose a speed limit within the Forest boundary and heavy fines for breaking it. The length of road involved is not great and it would not be difficult to enforce. But all attempts to have a speed limit imposed have failed. The Verderers have for years kept a detailed record of each accident involving a commonable animal and have marked on a map where it took place. It is noticeable from the information thus obtained that there are fewer accidents where there is an enclosure fence on one side of the road and still fewer where there is a fence on each side of the road. I should personally hate to see all the main roads in the Forest fenced—I would like to see a speed limit with really heavy fines imposed, and enforced, for exceeding it (but I realize that that is crying for the moon)—for this would drastically alter the scenic character of the Forest I have known and loved since childhood. But sooner or later all the main roads will, I am sure, be fenced.

All the pressures, it will be seen, are from outside the Forest. The 1947 Committee was well aware that there would be pressure from outside and did their best to plan for it. They could not, of course, foresee the extent of the pressure that would build up within twenty years of their investigation: the huge increase in population, the steady spread of the suburbs of such places as Bournemouth and Southampton, the greatly increased industrialization along Southampton Water, the fantastic increase in the numbers of visitors during the summer months, the vast increase in the volume of motorized traffic throughout the year. All these things have happened and the process will not stop: on the contrary, it will continue to gather momentum year by year. And these pressures have already affected the Forest to a degree which the 1947 Committee could not possibly have visualized.

We hear a great deal nowadays about "preserving the character of the Forest". But which character? The character of the Forest I knew in childhood and as a young man has altogether disappeared: and disappeared for all time. It can never be recovered. For that matter, the character of the Forest has been altered, and altered permanently, since the 1949 Act. It is no longer a question of "preserving the character of the Forest" (whatever that may mean), it is now a question of deciding what sort of Forest is wanted. And, that having been decided, taking the necessary steps to ensure that it is maintained, no matter what pressures are exerted from without.

This brings me back to the "rolling powers" for improvement which are enshrined in the 1949 Act. There can be no doubt at all that large areas of the Forest could be turned, reasonably quickly and with comparatively little trouble, into enclosed and profitable farms. The ploughing campaign during the last war proved that conclusively enough. There is no reason why land which has been reclaimed from heath—and today, as never before, it is possible to reclaim such land—should be allowed to revert to heath. All that would be necessary to prevent this would be to maintain the fences around the enclosed areas. As I say, there can be no doubt at all that large areas of the open Forest could now be transformed into good pasture. The reclaimed land would not, of course, provide cheap grazing (as the present grazing is), indeed it would be as dear as good grazing anywhere else, but there can be no doubt that such reclaimed land would be eagerly taken up.

Now, it may well seem ridiculous to contemplate the reclamation of large areas of the Forest and their transformation into fenced areas of reasonably good grazing land. The very idea will horrify those who have known and loved the Forest in the past. They will comfort themselves with the thought that, should any such revolutionary proposal be put forward, the Commoners would at once vote it down. But I think that there is every likelihood, in the not-distant future, of pressure from outside for such reclamation. Farmers on the Forest verges who watch their land being swallowed up by new housing estates may well begin to press for some measure of reclamation of the open Forest on their doorstep. And I do not think that it can any longer be assumed that the Commoners would automatically vote any such proposal down.

Undoubtedly the older generation of Commoners would have done so without the least hesitation. But the older generation of Commoners—the men who kept a cow or two, a pig or two, a few ponies; the men who exercised their Rights of Common and for whom those Rights existed—has virtually ceased to exist. It is here, on the Commoner, that pressure from outside has had its most important effect. And it is this pressure that has altered the whole character of the Forest.

No longer does every Commoner have his cow, his pig, his pony. The vast majority of those "small Commoners" who still live in the Forest—and many still do, of course—now go daily to work in the industries around the Forest borders. They earn good money. They no longer have any vital need to insist upon their Rights of Common. And it must be remembered that many have moved beyond the Forest boundaries to be nearer their work, to live (under the pressure of their womenfolk; and this a reflection of outside pressure) in more convenient modern houses. Their cottages have been taken over and turned into "desirable modern residences" by retired people, by the executive and managerial class working in near-by industry or working as far away as London. (Brockenhurst is now within the London commuter belt, within the first-class season ticket belt.) Much of the southern part of the Forest has within recent years become a dormitory area.

It is true, of course, that the Rights of Common have passed with these holdings to their new occupiers. But few of these new occupiers exercise these Rights (except, in some cases, in the case of ponies; and then not because the pony is valuable as a cash crop, as was the case with the genuine Commoner, but because it is valuable as a social symbol) and, probably, none of them have any vital interest in their maintenance. They still have the right to vote for an elective Verderer, of course. But, if present trends continue (and there is no reason to suppose that they will not; nor, indeed, that they will not accelerate), the elective Verderers will not, within the measurable future, be representing, as once they would have been, the interests of the "small Commoner". Inevitably, they will be representing more sophisticated interests; be subject to quite different pressures. It cannot safely be assumed that the elective Verderers in the future will automatically vote down any proposal for reclamation.

The virtual disappearance of the "small Commoner", and all he stood for, in the face of inexorable outside pressures is a factor of immense importance for the future of the Forest. I do not know how many small Commoners there are at present exercising their Rights of Common; perhaps no more than two hundred and fifty. You would not think so, judging by the numbers of cattle in the Forest. There are now probably four or five times as many cattle as ponies grazing the Forest. But the vast majority of these do not belong to the Commoners. They belong to a handful of men who are, in fact, "ranching" on a very considerable scale and at a very low cost. They turn their animals—the beef breeds do particularly well in the Forest—under licence from the Verderers. The annual fee is thirty shillings for each animal: very cheap grazing indeed.

One hears an increasing number of complaints nowadays— mostly from the new residents (who include, it should be remembered, the new Commoners)—about the numbers of cattle and ponies wandering at will in the Forest. These complaints show a truly lamentable ignorance of one basic fact: namely that grazing by the Commoners' animals—or, as it is now, by animals turned into the Forest under licence—is the only practicable way of keeping open the enormous areas of the Forest not enclosed by the Forestry Commission and so of providing the wide open spaces sought by both visitors and local people. It has been said that the ponies and the cattle are the architects of the Forest scenery. And this is true. Remove the cattle and the ponies, and the open areas of the Forest would very soon become impenetrable jungle and the roadside verges would disappear under scrub. And this would also be the case if the animals were to be confined to certain areas: with the added risk of disease. Of course, the open areas could be kept open by human agency. But the cost would have to be met from the rates: and the cost would be enormous. The present system is admirable from the point of view of the maintenance of the open Forest; and, at the same time, it provides a welcome, and not inconsiderable income, for the Verderers, an income which is put to good use. Indeed, if I have a complaint about the present system, it is that it is not used to the full. I would like to see many more cattle grazing the Forest under licence. I believe that it could probably carry as many as 8,000 head with advantage to the open Forest. At any rate, I am convinced that, no matter what the pressures from outside, it is only by the continuance of the present system—for the "small Commoner" is never again going to play a significant part—that the character of the Forest, as we know it today, can be maintained.

But the Forest is not merely a matter of trees and animals. The Forestry Commission can (and, of course, will) maintain their Inclosures, can (and, of course, will) carry out their other duties to the best of their ability; the "ranchers" can continue to turn their herds into the Forest by permission of the Verderers. But there are also people to be considered, both those that live in the Forest and those that come to it. If their interests are not taken fully into consideration, then nothing—nothing whatever—will "preserve" the Forest as we know it today.

This basic, and incontrovertible, fact seems to have been fully realized only by the New Forest Association of Parish Councils. This Association set up a Committee in December 1964 with the following terms of reference:

(A) To examine, and keep under review, the effect of the Green Belt on local villages and parishes.

(B) To reconcile the interests of local people and visitors, but at the same time to press for the improvement of the local tourist industry.

These terms of reference are most interesting. There is, you will notice, no mention of "preserving the character of the Forest". The emphasis is all upon people. And this emphasis is most significant.

Reading these terms of reference, one might come to the

conclusion that the preservation of the character of the Forest is of little interest, of little importance, to the local people. Of course, this is not the case. And this was made very plain in the Report of the Committee (composed of local men of long association with the Forest) which was published in July 1965 and which says:

> Change is inevitable. The forces are powerful and outside our control, but change will not necessarily spoil the New Forest. The more interest local people take in these changes, the more chance they can be channelled in the way we want and bring benefit to Forest people, and the less risk that the Forest as we know it will be spoilt. Ignoring the changes will not stop them. Others will direct and exploit them with scant regard for local interests.

Now, that is taking a good, hard look at the situation and its implications. And this is something which, it seems to me, has long been needed and something which the authority primarily responsible for the administration and well-being of the Forest has not yet been able to bring itself to do.

It has often been said that the New Forest faces the same problem as many of the wilder parts of Britain; the problem of tourism. People go to the wilder parts of Britain to escape the pressures of urbanization, in search of fresh air and solitude; a few to enjoy the beauties of unusual animal and plant life. And in the process they often destroy what they have come to enjoy. Of course, this is as true of the New Forest as elsewhere.

But the New Forest is faced with the problem in a much more severe form than any other wild part of Britain: in a much more severe form than, for example, Dartmoor or Exmoor. And this is because of its situation. By comparison, Dartmoor and Exmoor are isolated. The New Forest is within easy (and quick) reach of London by train, within a few minutes by car of Bournemouth and Southampton, lies across the main roads taking the through traffic to Bournemouth, Christchurch, Lymington and Poole, has an industrial belt developed and developing along its eastern border. The suburbs of Bournemouth and Lymington reach to the fringe of the Forest, and Southampton presses ever westward. Already Southampton has placed before the Local Government

Verderers Court

Commission proposals for the inclusion of parishes along the western shore of Southampton Water within its boundary in order to accommodate its overspill population. This proposal, if accepted (which is not unlikely), would mean the denial to the New Forest of the rateable assets of the vast refinery at Fawley, of the ancillary industries, and of the Marchwood generating station: a denial that would affect, adversely, everyone living within the Forest. Nor is there any certainty that the matter would end there, for in due course there will be another overspill population to accommodate. People, it will be realized, are of the utmost importance to the future of the Forest.

Within the Forest there is a "people problem". There is, at the moment, a Green Belt. I say "at the moment" because experience elsewhere has shown that Green Belts have a habit of shrinking and the New Forest Green Belt is unlikely to prove an exception. The Green Belt idea, here as elsewhere, is obviously an excellent one in principle. Nobody wants to see any large-scale housing development in the Forest. But the effect of Green Belt planning controls in the Forest is often to cause considerable hardship to people born and bred there. It is largely because of the effect of the Green Belt that village life as a distinct and continuing social entity is disappearing in the Forest and the villages, especially in the southern part, are fast becoming dormitory centres or places of retirement, largely populated by newcomers with no firm stake in the Forest. To prevent the continuance of this trend (which could have a disastrous effect on the Forest as a whole) it is suggested that light industry appropriate to Forest villages must be brought in to provide employment for married women, and for school-leavers and lower paid workers for whom the cost of commuting is really too high. It is also suggested that more houses, particularly council houses, are needed in the villages in order to keep young married people in the villages and to prevent them being forced out (as is often the case at present) by wealthier newcomers. This is also the case, of course, with elderly people, who are often unable to stay in their villages because of the weight of outside money.

These suggestions are so obviously sensible that one can only
13

Fawley Refinery

wonder why they have not been made before: why they had to be made by a Committee appointed by the New Forest Association of Parish Councils.

The other part of the "people problem" lies in the visitors. At the time of writing (1965) visitors are coming to the Forest at the rate of some two million a year. And there can be no doubt whatever that they are going to come in ever-increasing numbers. The propinquity of Bournemouth, Poole and Southampton, and the ever-increasing numbers of car-owners, make that inevitable. There is no way of preventing this influx. So long as the Forest is Crown land these visitors come by right.

Now, it is foolish to pretend that two million plus visitors a year do not affect the Forest. They do: and in innumerable ways. But these visitors may be divided into two classes: the campers and the day-visitors. The day-visitors outnumber the campers by at least a hundred to one, and it is the day-visitors who are the major danger to the general character of the Forest.

The Report suggests that, since the vast majority of visitors consider the Forest a "playground", "playground areas" should be established: parts of the Forest to which crowds could be attracted and where facilities such as traders, car parks and lavatories could be concentrated. This recommendation will horrify many people, who will consider that the establishment of such "playground areas" will ruin the character of the Forest. Personally, I think that if something on these lines is not done, and done quickly, the character of the Forest is going to be ruined by sheer weight of numbers. Certainly, if such areas were established and car-borne day-visitors encouraged to frequent them, the deep Forest would be additionally protected.

The deep Forest itself poses some problems. Obviously, it should, as far as possible, be kept in its wild state. If the unique fauna and flora of the Forest is to be protected, then large areas must be preserved from the invasion of car-borne picnickers. Entry by car should be forbidden; should be kept strictly for the more adventurous, the more energetic, the more studious. This is sound in principle, but might prove difficult to translate into practice. It must be remembered that severe restrictions will affect the local inhabitant no less than the day-visitor. The answer would seem to be the provision of good parking facilities at certain points on the fringes of the deep Forest and a complete ban on all cars within it. The ban would be easy enough to enforce—people are disinclined to take their cars over very rough tracks. Car parks on the fringes of the Forest would undoubtedly be unsightly, but there would not need to be very many of them and it should not be difficult to site them in such a way as not to interfere with the scenic character too drastically.

The camper should pose no problem at all. The problems that have arisen in connection with camping are born not of the camper as such, but of the Forestry Commission's attitude towards him. The Forestry Commission, it would seem, does not like the camper, *sui generis*. Camping is, at present, restricted (upon payment of a most reasonable fee: indeed, I think, much too low a fee) in certain areas. Since these areas are, in general, most inadequately serviced, have few (if any) amenities, most of them are by the end of the summer (and frequently well before then) in a disgusting state. But this is not, basically, the fault of the camper. It is the fault of the Forestry Commission and its "compound mentality". For that is what it amounts to: the campers are herded into compounds like the gypsies.

If this official attitude is maintained, disaster for the Forest must follow; for authority will, in due course, be flouted. The large towns are too close: two million plus visitors annually too many to be treated with a lofty disdain. There can be no doubt that more properly serviced camping sites will have to be provided (probably at slightly increased fees), for the numbers of caravan-campers will certainly continue to increase. The Forestry Commission may not like the idea, may not relish the prospect, but they will simply have to meet the demand.

The Report also has this to say:

As the Forest is one of the very few areas in Northern Europe where camping is possible anywhere (within reason) over a very large area, we consider this freedom is a valuable thing and should be preserved for those who prefer solitude to modern plumbing. Limited access

for car campers might be allowed to remote parts of the Forest, although denied to day visitors.

This suggestion—surely, a most reasonable one; for the man who
wishes to camp far from all the amenities, who genuinely wants
solitude, is the man who knows how to camp, the man who would
bury his litter, who would not risk fire, who would not be a
danger to anyone—was put to the Forestry Commission. It was
turned down: the "compound mentality" again.

The Report rightly calls for a complete change in local attitudes
towards tourists. It points out that the New Forest is a tourist area,
whether the locals like it or not, but that local authorities seem
reluctant to recognize the fact. In every other tourist area in the
world visitors are a major factor in the local economy. Great
efforts are made to attract them and to ensure that when they are
there, they have plenty of opportunity to spend their money. In
the New Forest, little or nothing is done to cultivate a great
potentiality. The Committee would like to see a New Forest
Tourist Board established, representing local authorities, the
Verderers, the Forestry Commission and other interested bodies.

I must confess that a few years ago I would, myself, have been
horrified at the very thought of a Tourist Board, at the very idea
of setting out to attract hordes of visitors with "playground areas"
and camping sites and the rest. But the visitors have come of their
own accord, and will continue to come in ever-increasing
numbers. And I am no longer horrified. On the contrary, I welcome all these suggestions and hope to see them translated into
fact.

It is true that the main roads through the Forest are going to get
more and more clogged. It is true that the two million visitors
annually will, in the not too distant future, become three million
visitors annually. But this does not necessarily mean that the
Forest and the "character" of the Forest will be spoilt. On the
contrary, if proper provision is made for these multitudes of
visitors—as, surely, it must be: at present, the Forestry Commission (perhaps naturally, in view of its main preoccupation)
cannot see the wood for the trees—then the Forest will benefit

greatly financially and the "character" of the Forest will be saved. For it is characteristic of the car-borne tourist to stick to the good roads—and there are not so many of them in the Forest—and to remain within easy reach of the amenities. Provide the amenities, carefully sited with this characteristic in mind, and vast areas of the open Forest, as wild and as lonely and as beautiful as ever, will be saved for those who know how to enjoy them—by walking the tracks and the pony paths.

The Forest has seen many changes through the centuries, experienced many vicissitudes. Today, it stands, I am convinced, on the threshold of a glorious and infinitely prosperous future.

It only needs someone to turn the key.

INDEX